MW01152052

FRENCH COUNTRY HIDEAWAYS

FRENCH COUNTRY HIDEAWAYS

VACATIONING AT PRIVATE CHÂTEAUS & MANORS IN RURAL FRANCE

Casey O'Brien Blondes

Photographs by Stephanie Cardon

RIZZOLI
NEW YORK

FRONT COVER:
Château de la Flocellière.
BACK COVER, FROM TOP:
Château de Ternay;
breakfast, Château des Réaux.
FRONT FLAP: *Guest room,*
Château de Saint-Loup.
PAGE 2: *Château d'Esparron.*
OPPOSITE: *Troglodyte house,*
Château des Ormeaux.

First published in the United States
of America in 2005
by Rizzoli International Publications, Inc.
300 Park Avenue South
New York, NY 10010
www.rizzoliusa.com

© 2005 Casey O'Brien Blondes

Photographs © 2005 Stephanie Cardon

All rights reserved. No part of this publication
may be reproduced, stored in a retrieval system,
or transmitted in any form or by any means,
electronic, mechanical, photocopying,
recording, or otherwise, without prior consent
of the publishers.

2005 2006 2007 2008 / 10 9 8 7 6 5 4 3 2 1

Designed by Karen Davidson

Printed in China

ISBN: 0-8478-2682-1

Library of Congress Control Number:
2005903043

ACKNOWLEDGMENTS

The most satisfying aspect of creating this book was the pleasure of working with a group of talented people who share a profound appreciation for French culture and the marvels of rural France. David Leddick, as ever, lit my way, and prodded me over the starting line. Adam Biro, Henri-Benoist Peres, and Alix de Saint Venant generously shared expertise and contacts. Chris Steighner at Rizzoli remained optimistic and supportive. Charlotte Sheedy nurtured at all the right moments, and Carolyn Kim ran through fire.

Stephanie Cardon produced a beautiful photographic record of thirty memorable encounters. Her artistry and cool intellect were invaluable resources throughout. The *French Country Hideaways* proprietors were uniformly gracious, forthcoming and hospitable—welcoming Stephanie and me into their homes and permitting us a remarkable degree of freedom. Karen Davidson expertly crafted an avalanche of content into an elegant book. Jeffrey Blondes provided a solution for every manner of difficulty and was a paragon of patience and support.

Thank you all.

FOR
DAVID
LEDDICK

"The French, at any rate,
living more slowly,
have learned the advantage
of living more deeply."

—EDITH WHARTON
French Ways and Their Meaning

FROM LEFT: *Normandy, Les Mille Feuilles; Loire, July poppies; Dordogne, drive into Château de Carbonneau; Provence, rosemary.*

INTRODUCTION

NOT LONG AFTER MY HUSBAND AND I MOVED FROM CONNECTICUT TO PARIS with our infant son in 1988, my in-laws treated us to a tour of the Loire Valley and Dordogne with stays at various château hotels. It was my first encounter with rural France and a welcome, pampered break from our cramped sublet apartment. I returned to the city smitten by the beauty of the landscapes we'd passed through, yet frustrated. I felt we'd merely glossed over culturally dense regions, without cracking their tourism veneer.

The sense of skimming, inherent in every rushed itinerary, was reinforced by the hotels where we stayed. Some were historic, most luxurious, yet all consistently impersonal. Meals in formal, well-staffed dining rooms, surrounded by other foreigners, had a generic consistency. The prospect of staying at a rural estate had conjured in my imagination a more textured, authentic experience. The reality was that these châteaus and manors were service establishments, not homes. They had long ceased to function as agricultural properties and consequently were severed from their roots. Once an estate is transformed into a hotel, its character is immediately compromised to satisfy the expectations of a demanding and diverse clientele.

I knew there had to be more satisfying alternatives. After all, France is blanketed with historic homes. Bertrand Le Nail, a leading historic property analyst who has done 2,500 appraisals and brokered the sale of 1,200 châteaus over thirty years, estimates that France has 40,000 châteaus, manor houses, and *gentilhommières*, over and above its 500 important historic châteaus. So I decided to seek out guest houses off the beaten path that retained a more authentic character. Happily, I

discovered that you no longer have to be a French aristocrat to experience life in a family-owned historic property. *French Country Hideaways* profiles a selection of my finds. It takes you on an insider's tour of private châteaus, manors, farms, and estates across some of France's most spectacular rural landscapes. The thirty family-owned bed-and-breakfasts featured have managed to preserve the spirit of a home while still providing a high level of service.

These B&Bs are part of a trend gaining momentum throughout France. More and more private estate owners are converting wings into gracious *chambres d'hôte* guest rooms. This arrangement is popular because it responds to the sophisticated traveler's desire for personalized hospitality. For proprietors, welcoming guests into their château is a means of economic diversification for properties that no longer get by on land-generated revenue and are too remote to attract substantial tourism for guided visits.

But the reasons for creating this type of B&B are not just economic. Over the years I've met and befriended many families in France who work hard to maintain and preserve their heritage. As dear to them as the buildings they've inherited or purchased is the surrounding landscape. The French tend to nurture country roots and many of the hosts you'll encounter have returned to manage a family property after a stint as an urban professional or living abroad.

Twelve years ago, I satisfied my own passion for country living by settling with our growing family and menagerie of animals in southern Touraine. The romantic wreck of a house we fell in love with evolved from a casual weekend getaway renovation to an ongoing opus. The magic has yet to wear off and I remain fascinated by the complexity of France's rural traditions and the splendor of its regional architecture. Far from exhausting my knowledge of the area, I've learned that another hidden treasure is always likely to be around the next corner.

In selecting the guest houses, my bias was authenticity and intimacy over grandeur and formality. I began with finds made through personal connections and a quest for places that exude quality and style. There is a range of amenities and pricing but every *maison d'hôte* here guarantees both the discovery of a living heritage and an encounter with the past. None of the destinations have more than a dozen guest rooms and most have fewer than six—to ensure you truly feel at home and benefit from your hosts' savoir faire while exploring their *pays*. An essential criterion in the selection process was a bond with the land—whether that means raising livestock, producing foie gras, or planting truffle oaks. Every destination is a haven from the hustle of routine where you can revel in the natural beauty of exceptional gardens, *potagers*, parks with rare specimen trees, forested hunting territory, vineyards, or acres of pasture and farmland. Because property owners are passionate about *produits du terroir*, most offer table d'hôte dinners featuring the best of local produce—frequently from their own property.

To get you started on travel research, each of the thirty proprietors has suggested a handful of *coups de coeur* (personal favorites)—an insider's list of recommended things to do and see within an hour's drive of their home. One of the highlights of your visit is sure to be sharing your hosts' incomparable knowledge of their region.

Every region has both a distinct personality and surprising diversity—in wine, cuisine, architecture, topography, and vegetation. Indigenous character is a reflection of subtle gradations in climate, altitude, and soil conditions—natural influences that shaped cultural identity and physical appearance over millennia.

It's no coincidence that France's western regions predominate: Brittany and Normandy; Loire, Vendée, and Berry; Dordogne and Aquitaine; and Provence. They remain some of the best-loved holiday destinations for foreigners and natives alike. They have retained a well-preserved rural character, escaped intense development, and are also where 70 percent of France's historic residences are to be found.

French Country Hideaways provides a glimpse behind the curtain at the lifestyle and traditions of property owners committed to perpetuating France's cultural heritage and their region's indigenous charm. It is a personal selection that is far from complete. I hope that it inspires your own tour of discovery.

BRITTANY & NORMANDY

BREST

St Malo

le Mont-St-Michel

La Ballue

B R E T A G N E

Guilguiffin

Quimper

RENNES

Rochefort-en-Terre

Vannes

Talhouët

THE REGIONS ON FRANCE'S PERIMETER tend to be singular and proudly independent. Brittany and Normandy are no exception. Outlying territories like the Basque country, Alsace, and Brittany historically had less contact with Paris and the golden mean of French civilization than with neighboring countries. Remove from the bureaucracy of a centralized state and the infusion of foreign influences fostered the regional languages and traditions that make them such compelling places to visit.

Brittany and Normandy—jutting northwest into the English Channel and Atlantic Ocean—were perhaps cut off from the capital but sustained ancient and enduring links with island neighbors to the north. Traveling through Normandy's picturesque Pays d'Auge, where timbered houses and thatched roofs abound, one is reminded of rural English counties, and a similar sense of déjà vu occurs in Brittany, where gray

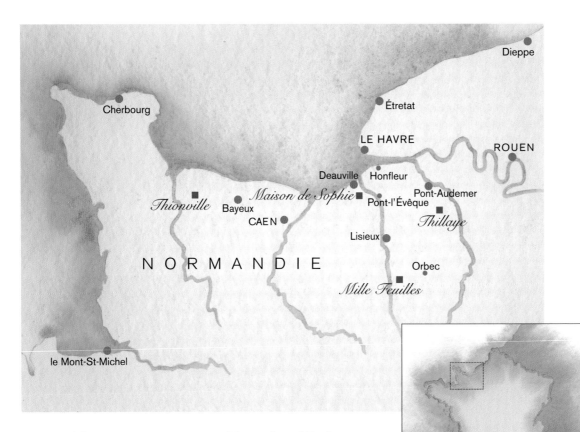

granite châteaus are reminiscent of Scottish and Irish manors.

The physical appearance of indigenous residents is also similar to northern European's—nowhere else in France are you likely to find such a concentration of blue eyes. The temperate influence of the sea, high annual rainfall, and peaty soil favor acid-loving hydrangeas, rhododendrons, and azaleas—just as they do in Ireland.

While neighbors with a contiguous coastline, Brittany and Normandy have contrasting and complementary personalities. Brittany is the rugged individualist, with craggy windswept shores, invincible granite architecture, salty maritime lore, and hardy rural temperament. The ubiquitous oyster is a fine symbol for Brittany—rough and hard-edged, tricky to pry open, creating a cool and salty first impression, followed by an inexplicably satisfying memory. An acquired taste once savored becomes an enduring passion.

Due east, Normandy is all soft curves and creamy cheeses. The staples of its rich but no-nonsense cuisine are apples and cream. The pink-cheeked Norman, glowing with health from a steady diet of Camembert and cider, is the enduring image that clings to the collective imagination.

The archetypal Norman landscape is most readily found in the rolling pastureland and wooded valleys of the Pays d'Auge and Calvados. The four Norman property selections here are clustered in this idyllic region between Bayeaux and Pont-Audemer, a brief drive inland from Honfleur, Deauville, and the Normandy landing beaches.

Pays d'Auge is among France's most pristine landscapes. The villages of timbered and brick houses are impeccably preserved and the countryside is a patchwork of emerald pastures edged with hedgerows, horse farms, manicured estates, and acres of apple orchards. Since the nineteenth century, Normandy has remained a favored Parisian retreat, with some of France's pricier real estate—driven up by competing demand from across the channel.

The Norman coastline stretches more than 370 miles and is dotted with innumerable boating harbors and sandy beaches. Other holiday destinations include 80 parks and gardens, 200 museums, and 39 golf courses. Normandy's creative peak occurred during the nineteenth century when painters and

PAGE 12, CLOCKWISE FROM TOP: *Auge Valley, Normandy; Beaumont-en-Auge boutique; Breton hydrangeas; Mont-Saint-Michel.* BELOW, FROM LEFT: *General store, Normandy; Calvados apples.* PAGE 16, FROM TOP: *Norman half-timbered houses, Pont-l'Évêque; old* fromagerie *(cheese shop) sign, Beauvron-en-Auge.*

FROMAGES

writers such as J. F. Millet, Eugène Boudin, Gustave Flaubert, and Guy de Maupassant attained national reputations. Today, Deauville's film festival is a major international cultural event.

In contrast, Brittany's isolation persisted well into the twentieth century, when highways first linked the peninsula to the interior. It has a long-held national reputation as a backward rural anomaly. The fictional Becasine, with her folkloric apron and inimitable *coiffe* headdress, epitomizes the stereotype of Bretons as naïve rural innocents. While Brittany's French literacy rate lagged below the national average, the Breton regional language thrived. It is now proudly spoken by over two hundred thousand natives and is increasingly taught in regional schools as an accredited second language.

A Celtic strain runs through Breton culture and is especially felt in the westernmost department of Finistère. Brittany's identity is inextricably bound to the sea. It is France's naval and fishing capital and the birthplace of its most celebrated sailors. Seafood, especially oysters, is a regional specialty.

Farming is an essential component of the Breton economy, and the interior produces much of France's potatoes, broccoli, beets, and leeks. Butter is the star of Breton gastronomy and the key to its reputation for mouthwatering cakes and biscuits. Crêpes are a staple, and once you've tasted them here with a *bol de cidre*, it will be hard to settle for gluey imitations.

The northernmost of the Brittany destinations, Mont-Saint-Michel, is symbolically located on the shifting sand border between the two regions. Though consensus currently gives the prize to Normandy, the dividing line cuts across the sacred isle. The Châteaus of Talhouët and Guilguiffin are parallel to Brittany's southern shore west of Nantes, which makes them equally accessible from a departure point in the western Loire.

Despite its off-the-track location, Brittany is unmatched for bracing character and intensity of emotion. Few leave indifferently, some leave resistantly, and most leave fervently promising to return. ❧

BELOW: *Breton granite façade, Rochefort-en-Terre.*

Château de Guilguiffin

GRANITE GRANDEUR

Guilguiffin lies within the *Pays Bigoudin* at the western limit of the Finistère peninsula, a region that symbolizes Breton culture in the popular imagination. Women here of a certain generation continue to proudly wear the traditional *coiffe*—an improbably tall lace headdress with trailing ribbons. The indigenous Breton language and music, with their Gaelic timbre, have experienced a popular revival. Road signs posted in French and Breton are a reminder that you have entered Celtic territory, where climate, vegetation, and native stone are reminiscent of southwest Ireland.

The Guilguiffin estate is one of the most distinguished historic properties in western Brittany. The current château is the latest aristocratic residence to have occupied the site since 1010. The Marquis of Ploec built it as a hunting retreat in the reign of Louis XV, with stones from the ruins of a fortified residence. Its ground-floor salons and first-floor guest suites retain an authentic eighteenth-century character with a lively color register of paintwork and fabrics. Double doors, once intended to keep out the cold, are now a guarantee of privacy.

The scale of everything at Guilguiffin is unmistakably grand. The immense stone-flagged entry hall, monumental double staircase, and filigree-iron balustrade have the imprimatur of stately home. In summer the hall becomes a contiguous indoor/outdoor space with the front terrace. Guests can linger over a drink while savoring the view across the *cour d'honneur* (main courtyard), ringed with remarkable stone columns inspired by the temple of Angkor-Vat.

Philippe & Angelika Davy's
COUPS DE COEUR

Finistère Coastline

An astounding variety of coastal landscape is within a ten- to twenty-five-minute drive. Dramatic cliffs, rocky creeks, and sandy beaches provide maritime scenery for every taste.

River Ports

The southern shore is fissured with coastal rivers harboring port villages. Two of the most scenic rivers are the Aven River near Pont-Aven (where Gauguin painted) and the Odet River near Saint Marine.

Guilvinec Fish Market

The port of Guilvinec is a bustling spectacle when fishing boats dock for the day and the race is on to get the catch to the wharf for wholesale auctions.

Presqu'île de Crozon and Parc Naturel Regional d'Armorique

North of Guilguiffin is a protected peninsula designated a state park. Ménez-Hom is an exceptional vantage point with a 30-mile view in all directions.

Local Restaurants

The area has an unusual concentration of small, high-quality restaurants offering diners a range of choice and good value, whether your taste runs to a casual crêperie, port-side fish restaurant, or gourmet menu.

(The architect had traveled extensively in the east.) Beyond one will find lawns, gardens, a formal pool, horse pastures, and acres of wooded parkland with meticulously tended alleys.

Equestrians are encouraged to trailer their horses to Guilguiffin to profit from 11 kilometers of bridle paths and to gallop along the sandy coastal beaches. Equine accommodation is excellent. Roomy stalls with adjoining paddocks are located just a five-minute walk from the house. There is also an excellent riding school nearby for those wanting to take lessons or to hire a horse and ride out with a guide.

Your host, Philippe Davy, is a man of abundant energy, and his sunny wife Angelika keeps up the pace with ease. Philippe is proud to note that the ground floor of the château, surrounding common buildings, and 111 acres of parkland are a protected historic zone. Fortunately he has the temperament needed for overseeing the considerable maintenance. After a career as a fighter pilot, Philippe trained as an architect specializing in historic restoration. Like five of the château's previous owners, he acquired the property through marriage. The son of a distinguished diplomat, Philippe is expert at putting his international guests at ease and has a particular affinity for Americans, since his son immigrated to Virginia to run

a stable and train fox hunters. Philippe is that rare breed of gentleman—as much at ease discussing the thousands of trees and hydrangea bushes he's planted as the intricacies of foreign affairs.

Guilguiffin might well qualify for a Guinness record for plantings—350,000 daffodils, thousands of azaleas and rhododendrons, and 30,000 hydrangeas have been put in. The grounds are an enchantment for flower lovers from February through October. 🍂

Château de Talhouët

A COLLECTOR'S PRIDE

The sober granite facade of this sixteenth-century Morbihan manor belies the comfort and refinement of its luxurious decor. Jean-Pol Soulaine is an indulgent proprietor, and Talhouët is a testament to his wonderful collector's eye. The felted ambiance of the salon, with its warm-hued eighteenth-century paneling, Renaissance beams, and elaborately carved fireplace, tempts guests to settle into a sofa and savor the harmony of carefully edited objects, pictures, and furnishings.

Talhouët first captivated Jean-Pol when he visited as an eight-year-old with his father, a neighboring lumber merchant. The former fiefdom of the Talhouëts, a noble Breton family, was already sliding into disrepair. When he began a search for a suitable B&B property some thirty years later, he was thrilled to find it on the market. Essential restoration accomplished, Jean-Pol began receiving guests fifteen years ago. The task of restoration and renewal of decor continues unabated.

Jean-Pol delights in creating a cozy and relaxing getaway destination for a loyal clientele. Nothing makes him happier than guests from the provincial city of Rennes, just twenty miles away, booking for dinner and an overnight stay. "They want to take full advantage of the house, rather than rushing back and forth for a meal. It allows them to relax in front of the fire and sleep in late."

Jean-Pol Soulaine's COUPS DE COEUR

Rochefort-en-Terre

Talhoeut is a five-minute drive from one of Brittany's most picturesque towns. Since Alfred Klotz, an American portraitist, rebuilt the château in 1910, it has become a community for artists and artisans. A stroll through the old center with its harmonious carved granite facades and unusual hand-crafted signage is a must.

Vannes

This is the gateway city to the Gulf of Morbihan, which is an enclosed sea reputed to contain as many islands as days of the year. A boat excursion with stop-offs at Ile d'Az and Ile aux Moines is recommended. The Wednesday and Saturday morning market is another highlight.

Les Remparts Antique Shop, Vannes

Pascale Brion and David Balzeaux have created "one of the loveliest boutiques in the west," according to Jean-Pol.

Kerouzine Cheese Shop, Vannes

An incomparable selection of France's finest farm cheeses can be found in this popular store in Vannes.

Josselin

A classic Breton village on the canal that runs from the port of Brest to the city of Nantes, Josselin is the location of the magnificent Gothic Château de Rohan.

The felted ambiance of the salon, with its warm-hued eighteenth-century paneling, Renaissance beams, and elaborately carved fireplace, tempts guests to settle in a sofa and savor the harmony of carefully edited objects, pictures, and furnishings.

Dinner is served seven days a week in the high season—July through September—and on weekends or upon request the rest of the year. This degree of service is a rarity for establishments of Talhouët's size and rural location. Chef Olivier Guyon, a native of the city of Nantes, has run the kitchen for seven years. His flavorful, unpretentious cuisine highlights the abundance of local fish and farm-fresh produce. Desserts are a particular specialty.

Protected by twenty acres of parkland and forest, guests are assured of total tranquility. All of the spacious guest rooms have a splendid view over garden or countryside. Low running granite walls define the five terraced gardens. Each has its particular character, ranging from classic French clipped yew topiaries to English-style mixed borders or a field of wildflowers.

As a Morbihan native and inveterate connoisseur of fine things, Jean-Pol is the ideal guide to his historic coastal region. ❧

Château et Jardins de La Ballue

MANNERIST MODERN

The Baroque gardens of Château de la Ballue have the distinction of being designated a National Historic Monument—not as a copy or restoration of historic gardens but as a contemporary creation in the spirit of seventeenth-century mannerism. As conceptual gardens, the botanic characteristics of the plants themselves are secondary to the architectural effect they create. Of primary importance are harmonies of light and shadow, the notion of surprise and overall refinement of composition. The aesthetic conquest of nature is the essence of the *jardin à la française,* and the gardens of La Ballue are the evolution of a formal symmetrical style exemplified in the seventeenth-century designs of Le Nôtre.

The classical terrace garden conceived by François Hébert-Stevens, nephew of modernist master Malley Stevens, is a sculpted chessboard of yews and hornbeam clipped to perfection. While intended for contemplation from the perspective of a window, viewed from the exterior the geometric parterre enhances the rigorous symmetry of the château's granite facade.

A yin/yang alley of twenty-two wisterias wended around columns of yew separates the classical parterre from the mannerist garden, which features thirteen "surprise" chambers laid out by Paul Maymont in 1973. An evergreen Temple of Diana, revealed beyond a row of lime trees, is a topiary marvel. Upon request, co-proprietor Alain Schrotter gives an excellent guided tour that illuminates the symbolic and allegorical dimension of the design, with commentary on the

Marie-France Barrère & Alain Schrotter's
COUPS DE COEUR

Walking Tour of Mont-Saint-Michel

From April to November walking tours of the island (accessible on foot via a bridge) are organized by the abbey and can be booked at the ticket office. It is also possible to tour the island at low tide on horseback. The extreme tidal currents around the island are the strongest in Europe.

Les Senteurs des Douaniers of the Emerald and Pink Granite Coasts

Coastal paths formerly used as lookouts by customs agents are now choice routes for scenic walks. The coastline between the towns of Cancale and Saint-Malo is especially well preserved.

Olivier Roellinger Restaurant

The best in Brittany, this top-rated restaurant for imaginative cuisine has unforgettable seafood.

Flat Oysters (Huîtres Plats) of Cancale

This distinctive variety of local oyster has hints of almond and pepper. Most of Cancale's seafood restaurants serve them fresh from their own parc à huîtres (oyster beds).

Lieu-Dit Contemporary Art Gallery

Lieu-Dit organizes four exhibitions per year, one per season. Open daily from 2 p.m. to 8 p.m. throughout exhibition periods and by appointment at other times. Located off the Hédé exit on the main road between the cities of Saint-Malo and Rennes.

contemporary sculpture collection displayed throughout.

Major writers and artists, inspired by its ambiance, have long frequented La Ballue. In the nineteenth century it was a favored destination for romantic period writers Victor Hugo, Balzac, and Châteaubriand. More recently, contemporary artists Takis, Tal-Coat, Rauschenberg, and Monory have worked there.

Marie-France Barrère and Alain Schrotter, fellow book publishers and former gallerists, purchased the property in 1995 after a decade in which it was abandoned. They restored and elaborated the gardens, respecting the modernist vision outlined in the 1970s design, and renovated the house to receive guests. Alain and Marie-France succumbed immediately to the La Ballue spell. Alain describes with a wry smile how "a château is a lot like a boat—it's a very self-contained environment. Ballue takes you in its arms and doesn't want to let you go. When you leave, you feel torn."

In keeping with the property's artistic heritage, Marie-France and Alain continue to promote the work of contemporary writers, artists, and musicians. The interior is filled with paintings, sculpture, ceramics, glass, and works on paper by a myriad of contemporary creators, many of whom are inspired by the mannerist tradition.

The ground-floor salons are furnished with an eclectic mix of modern, Art Deco, and antique pieces. Alain detects an echo of Baroque sensibility in the Art Deco period, which in turn influenced recent neo-Baroque design. First-floor guest rooms are themed to evoke their distinctive personalities. Canopied beds are a recurrent feature, and several rooms with paneling have been inventively fitted with eighteenth-century-inspired *cabinets de toilette* (bathrooms), with contemporary fixtures.

Bridging the frontier of Normandy and Brittany, La Ballue is a twenty-minute drive from the island of Mont-Saint-Michel. Architecturally, the château is decidedly Breton in feel. The influence of Italian mannerism is a

legacy of Brittany's former linen industry, which engendered an exclusive trading partnership with Italy in the seventeenth century and corresponding cultural exchange. Alain is fascinated by this privileged link: "Baroque didn't exist in France beyond Brittany. Louis XIV threw Gian Bernini out, so the influence of the counter-reform movement begun by Michelangelo was confined to Brittany."

The bond with Italy remains. "Mont-Saint-Michel is a traditional honeymoon destination for Italians, much as Venice is for us. We receive lots of Italian newlyweds." But you don't have to be on a honeymoon to enjoy a romantic idyll at this majestic granite retreat, filled with sensory and intellectual stimulation. 🍂

Manoir de Thionville

AN ARTIST'S VISION

Thionville is a tranquil, intimate base from which to explore the cultural and historic riches of Calvados. The apple orchards, pastureland, and sandy shores of this deceptively bucolic region have witnessed a thousand years of historic drama—from the Norman conquest of Britain retold in the eleventh-century tapestries on display in Bayeux, to the D-day landing at Omaha Beach. There is plenty to satisfy the whims of history buffs, nature lovers, and amateurs of first-rate regional produce. Nicole and Michel Fernando are attentive, stimulating hosts, who steer visitors beyond the banal to ensure a memorable stay.

Cuisine is a focal point at Thionville. Energetic Michel cultivates a bounty of fresh produce in his decorative *potager,* and the gracious and discreet Nicole scouts the finest local ingredients for simple and savory table d'hôte dinners.

A native of Bayeux, Nicole has a deep attachment to Normandy. Marriage and career took her to Paris but the couple purchased Thionville as a country retreat two decades ago. The dreamy landscape of marsh and pastureland surrounding the house was the perfect antidote to the hustle of professional life in Paris—where Michel ran a children's clothing company and Nicole a linens and furnishings boutique at Place des Vosges. On weekends the big house filled with guests, and Nicole harbored a dream of returning to live there full-time once their daughters were grown.

Two years ago, she got her wish when they sold their home in the city and undertook full renovation of the

Nicole & Michel Fernando's COUPS DE COEUR

Les Marais

A magical expanse of marshland at the confluence of three rivers is a ten-minute bike ride from the village of Colombières toward Trevières. Irrigation by dikes has created pasture for cows, which share the natural reserve with herons, storks, and water iris. During ten days each June, a multitude of frogs stage an unforgettable concert of croaks at sundown.

Baie des Veys

Six and a half miles west beyond Isigny (famed for its incomparable butter) lies a magnificent bay irrigated by two rivers. The marshy landfill ringing the shore is a peaceful no-man's-land and nature lovers' paradise.

Historic Bayeux

A lively medieval festival animates the well-preserved town center the first week of July—featuring improvised skits by costumed actors and re-creation of old guilds. Don't miss the splendid Gothic Cathedral of Notre-Dame and its crypt.

Omaha Beach

Nicole enjoys walking the dogs along the vast expanse of sand at this nearby beach. The sole company you're likely to encounter is a horse from a neighboring haras (horse farm) out on a training run.

Fishing villages of Barfleur and Saint Vaast-la-Houge

The villages are up the coast past Utah Beach. Visit the home and atelier of nineteenth-century artist Paul Signac and the landmark Gosselin épicerie (gourmet shop), where chic Parisians stock up on distinctively packaged delicacies.

previously neglected wing of the manor. For these two aesthetes with a mania for detail, the project became an all-consuming occupation for eighteen months. The result is a handsomely subtle decor with a focus on texture, patina, and the luster of natural materials. Wherever possible, surfaces have been stripped to reveal natural finish. Original wattle and daub were uncovered beneath plaster in the stairwell, and decorative cast-iron radiators were restored to working order. Walking through the renovated guest wing, one can't resist the sensual pleasure of running a hand along a polished banister or stone mantelpiece. The three guest rooms are minimally but carefully furnished, and spacious bathrooms have been handsomely refitted with retro-style contemporary fixtures.

A career dealing with clients and entertaining weekend guests convinced Nicole she was well suited for her new lifestyle. She especially enjoys it when guests eat in, as it creates an opportunity to get to know them better. "My friends ask me why we didn't opt for the freedom of running a *gîte* (self-catering rental) but I prefer the human contact that a small bed-and-breakfast provides."

The grounds are Michel's domain. He recently planted a formal *jardin à la française* with a geometric interplay of lawn, flowerbeds, and fruit trees within the square plot of ground formed behind the perpendicular wings of the house. The front and side gardens are graced with mature trees, flowering bushes, and clambering roses, forming shady nooks for a quiet read or siesta. The homey ambiance of Thionville encourages visitors to settle in and relax, stop off for a visit at Michel's light-filled painting atelier, or simply wander the wooded glade with its carpet of mauve cyclamens.

La Maison de Sophie

YOUR WISH IS GRANTED

In the eighteenth century, Marie Antoinette created a fantasy Norman village at Versailles where she escaped the formality of court to play the role of milkmaid in an idealized farmyard. Sophie Dudemaine, France's reigning queen of cake (her best-selling cookbook *Les Cakes de Sophie* has sold over one million copies), updated the fantasy when she quit Paris for a storybook village in the Pays d'Auge and created a guest house consecrated to comfort and cuisine.

The former presbytery resembles a giant Georgian dollhouse. Rows of generous windows accentuate the perfect symmetry of its washed brick facade. The sunny interior has a decor to match, with a light touch in fabrics and furnishings. Guests may choose one of four themed guest rooms: the ultra-trendy Zen, the airy exoticism of Marrakech, the romantic femininity of Victoria, or the nautical cheer of Deauville (a reminder that the chic coastal resort is but ten minutes north). For children, there is a toy-filled roost under the eaves, which accommodates up to five preteens.

Sophie describes her guest house as a *maison ludique* or playhouse. Families with young children are welcome, although Sophie is sensitive about lodging them with couples. If a young family books in, couples seeking an escape on their own are duly cautioned.

The main attractions here are table d'hôte cuisine and Sophie's cooking ateliers, which are themed according to season, holidays, and local produce. The kitchen is a focal point of activity, where guests tend to congregate. The

Sophie Dudemaine's
COUPS DE COEUR

Val de Cimes Adventure Forest

This novel obstacle course through trees involves high wires, plank bridges, and tyrolien (Alpine) slings. A safe but exhilarating forest adventure for all age and nerve levels, the forest has platform height ranges from 6 feet for small children up to 36 feet for the fearless.

Château du Vendeuvre Museum and Gardens

The Vendeuvre family château appeals to every age. You'll find eighteenth-century furnishings, the world's most extensive miniature furniture collection, a survey of period dog beds and kennels, and lavish grounds with architectural follies and water features.

Escargots de Brotonne

This curious snail farm near the town of Pont Audemer is fascinating to visit at night when the nocturnal creatures are active.

La Ferme des Bruyères—Authentic Cider and Local Produce

This is Sophie's preferred address for stocking up on Pays d'Auge apple treats: cider, pommeau (a blend of apple cider juice and Calvados), Calvados, vinegar, juice, jams, cider jelly, and more.

Village of Beaumont en Auge

A five-minute drive from La Maison de Sophie is one of the timeless villages that give this region its reputation for charm and authenticity. There is a fine view of the Auge Valley at the edge of the town square and an abundance of lovingly preserved homes and shops with indigenous timbered facades, patterned brickwork, and slate detailing.

ambiance is homey and bright, with red and yellow tiles and hand-painted cabinetry featuring farmyard vignettes by artist Vivianne Douek. This is Sophie's laboratory/salon, where she's in her element testing recipes and sharing her savoir faire. It's also the backdrop for her program on *Cuisine TV*.

A row of crayon-bright children's aprons underscores attention paid to young guests. Children are encouraged to participate in the weekend brunch atelier, where they prepare their own cakes, crêpes, and assorted treats. Another family-friendly feature is child meals served in the kitchen. This allows adults the luxury of a relaxed dinner while kids explore the cache of games and DVDs, visit the petting zoo, or burn off steam in the mini adventure-playground.

Beyond hard work and talent, Sophie's success results from a refusal to be stymied by French cooking convention. "Authenticity, simplicity and originality" is her motto. It is also an apt description of the woman, whose considerable ingenuity transformed a baking business, begun in her kitchen with distribution at local markets, into a fast-growing gourmet empire.

Sophie's cookbooks are pleasing to the eye. Written for time-pressed housewives and dual-career couples, they feature basic ingredients and home-tested recipes sprinkled with corner-cutting tips. Alain Ducasse, a high priest of French haute cuisine, is so intrigued by the appeal of Sophie's cookbooks with their unpretentious photos and straight-talking text that she's helping him reformulate his classic recipes for the casual chef.

Always seeking new ways to entertain and pamper her clientele, Sophie has introduced sewing and gardening workshops and a range of grooming and spa services. The sole drawback to the plethora of temptations is finding the time to enjoy them all. ✄

Les Mille Feuilles

BOCAGE BOHÈME

Pierre Brinon is a wizard when it comes to ambiance. Given a hodgepodge of thrift-shop furniture, bolts of fabric, cans of paint, garden greenery, and a smattering of eccentric *objets*, he'll conjure up an interior worthy of a decorating magazine spread. Which is why Les Mille Feuilles à la Campagne has animated the pages of chic international publications since its opening in 2002. Brinon's style is a theatrical hybrid of baroque-meets-junk-chic with Bloomsbury overtones.

Romantic lighting enhances the mood, and candles are everywhere. Sipping a glass of Bordeaux by the fire in the winter salon on a bracing October evening, you feel as though you've been invited to a private club. Pierre is busy preparing dinner in the cavernous yet cozy kitchen. Having run a restaurant, he is at ease using yet another of his creative talents. "Inventive but not eccentric" is how Pierre describes the menu. Specialties include *terrine de courgettes*, pungent with cheese from the neighboring village of Livarot; *poulet Vallée d'Auge* with apples and cider; seven-hour leg of lamb; codfish with grapefruit and mango; and a mouth-watering savarin yeast cake garnished with crème frâiche and garden blackberries.

The old-walled *potager* supplies vegetables and the orchard more apples than he finds use for. Amusingly, Pierre's *basse-cour* (poultry yard) provides eggs for the neighboring farmer. "The fox raided her henhouse one too many times. Now she's happy to get her eggs from the city boy next door."

Pierre Brinon's
COUPS DE COEUR

Lisieux Market
The Saturday morning market of this regional center remains authentic, with small local suppliers offering live chickens, farm-fresh dairy products, and flowers direct from their gardens.

The Fish Shop in Orbec
Pierre is an ardent fan of the two women who run a first-rate fishmonger in the neighboring village. They're up at dawn to source the freshest catch from the Norman coast and are ever ready with a recipe.

Antique Fair in
Saint Pierre sur Dives
The first Sunday of every month, the village's fifteenth-century covered market shelters scores of brocante (flea market) stalls. Pierre found many of his treasures there.

Annual Lisieux Tree Fair
A five-hundred-year-old tradition is staged the first week of March for three days. Half the town is closed to traffic to make way for a forest of saplings of every description, with a particular focus on fruit trees.

Manoir Coupe Sarte
A masterpiece of indigenous timbered Pays d'Auge architecture, this sublime sixteenth-century manor house is ringed by a moat. Infrequently open to the public, it is still worth a visit to admire the setting and craftsmanship of its facade.

Pierre Brinon is a restless creative spirit with entrepreneurial instincts. His other job is keeping an eye on his two successful floral design shops in Paris's Marais district. After fifteen years in the business, a solid reputation, and six franchised Les Mille Feuilles boutiques in Japan, Pierre was ready for another challenge. "After working with flowers so many years, I feel like there's little more I can do for them." His book *Leçons de Fleurs* (*Flower Lessons*), published by Flammarion and co-authored with Philippe Landri, is a fabulous summary of his floral design skill.

The launch of Pierre's bed-and-breakfast project was serendipitous. He owned a weekend home in the area and began to look around for something more unusual. He came upon the Domaine de la Petit Lande estate three days before it was to go up for auction and decided immediately it had to be his. The nineteenth-century pink stucco *maison bourgeoise* had been in steady decline over several decades. Built as a secondary residence by a wealthy industrialist from the north, its vacation home style and north/south orientation are atypical of the region. In its heyday, the house and multiple outbuildings were considered a model farm property. The novel fire-heated greenhouse, irrigation system, and reinforced concrete silo were the height of modernity. By the time Pierre took ownership, the roof over the dozen maids' rooms was leaking water into forty-five strategically placed pails. Pierre saw only potential and, after nine months of furious renovation, was ready to receive. He recently purchased back the *métairie* (small farm) next door and has a scheme to transform it and a disused cider house into two self-catering guest houses. "It's gratifying to watch the house recover its lost luster, and decline purchase offers from Parisian clients, who come for a weekend and want to make it as their own." ❧

Château la Thillaye

TOP-FLIGHT HOSPITALITY

La Thillaye creates a magnificent impression, glimpsed through the trees as you drive into the secluded 69-acre park sheltering this impeccably maintained Louis XIII château. The patterned brickwork highlighted with creamy stone, sturdy turrets capping the facade, and slate roof are hallmarks of a classic Norman castle.

While isolated enough to ensure tranquility, the property is just one and a half hours from Paris, twenty minutes from the coastal port of Honfleur, and within tantalizing reach of twenty international-caliber golf courses. The lawn flanking the château is but a preview of Normandy's flawless greens. The region is France's golf Valhalla, and La Thillaye is a restful meeting place to unwind after a day out on the links or touring the gamut of neighboring historic and cultural attractions.

Roxanne Longpré and Patrick Matton manage their property with admirable professionalism, providing the intimacy of a family-owned establishment with service one might expect at a luxury hotel. Attention to detail is Roxanne's mantra and she goes out of her way to give guests' needs her personal attention.

A native of Quebec, Roxanne met her French husband when they both lived and worked in Montreal. Patrick moved to Canada from Burgundy as a young hotel-school graduate and spent his career as a hotel and banquet chief for projects like the Olympic Stadium and the historic port of Montreal. Roxanne managed one of Montreal's major international fairs for seventeen years. Their combined service and travel experience resulted in extensive personal wish lists for dream

Roxanne Longpré & Patrick Matton's
COUPS DE COEUR

Abbey of Notre Dame du Bec
This peaceful abbey founded in 1034 is home to an industrious religious community. Classic painted faience pottery crafted by the monks is sold in a well-stocked shop, which offers the possibility of customized orders for dinner services or wedding gifts.

Honfleur
This charming harbor is a popular destination for browsing galleries and touring the picturesque quays. Eugene Boudin, a pioneer of the Impressionist movement, lived and painted here. It is also the birthplace of avant-garde composer Erik Satie. Both have museums dedicated to their work.

Champ de Bataille Golf Club, Château, and Gardens
Roxanne recommends Champ de Bataille because of its proximity to the adjacent château and gardens, extensively refurbished by haute decorator Jacques Garcia. There's something for everybody, when half of a couple doesn't play golf.

Pont-Audemer
In the Venice of Normandy, just 5 miles north of La Thillaye, canals fed by the Risle River crisscross the old town center. Don't miss the twice-weekly market on Monday and Friday mornings.

Indian Summer Weekends
Offered October through February, this event is themed around a wealth of gastronomic products produced from native apples.

Roxanne Longpré and Patrick Matton manage their property with admirable professionalism, providing the intimacy of a family-owned establishment with service one might expect at a luxury hotel.

accommodation, so when Patrick felt the urge to return to his French roots, Roxanne encouraged him to commit to a project that would make best use of their professional experience and multicultural sensitivities.

La Thillaye formerly encompassed several thousand acres of property and was considered among the premiere estates of the Haute-Normandie region. Built in 1645 by Nicolas Pillon du Coudray, it remained in the original family until the twentieth century. The celebrated architect Lenormand was responsible for a harmonious facelift of the rear facade. The extensive renovation undertaken by the current owners included total restoration of the central stairwell, heavily damaged by fire in the 1920s, and the refurbishment of spacious bedrooms with well-appointed modern bathrooms. The top floor has two large suites with views overlooking the front and rear grounds.

There is plenty of room inside and out for solitude. The estate has gracefully landscaped lawns planted with specimen trees and flowering bushes, and the woods have kilometers of cleared paths for nature walks. The spacious reception rooms are well arranged, with separate seating areas. A library—well stocked with English and French language titles—bridges the music room and grand salon. Its shelf of auction house catalogs and art and antiques books is testimony to Patrick's avowed weakness for collectibles. He sold a good portion of them to finance

restoration of La Thillaye but he has no regrets. The guest and reception
rooms are decorated with his print collection.

Patrick currently channels his aesthetic flair into cuisine for table d'hôte
dinners. The menu is quite sophisticated, and North American influence is
reflected in the generosity of his portions and a twist on traditional French
recipes. The ambiance of the dining room, where guests may eat at separate
tables, is refined. For families or groups, there is an informal country-style
dining room with a large table, which doubles as the breakfast room.

Patrick notices a growing demand for restaurant service. "Most guests
come to relax and don't want to get in their car and drive somewhere in the
evening. Dining here lets them enjoy a of bottle of wine and leisurely meal
without worrying about getting back."

Roxanne has developed a program of themed weekends, which promote
the unique character of the property. One of the more unusual offers is
the possibility of organizing a "shooting" weekend from late September
through February, which permits guests the opportunity to participate in
a traditional French hunt. The wooded park at La Thillaye has a mix of
small and large game—from woodcock, partridge, and rabbit to wild boar.
Licensed hunters are encouraged to book well in advance to arrange for
a temporary French permit. ❧

LOIRE, VENDÉE & BERRY

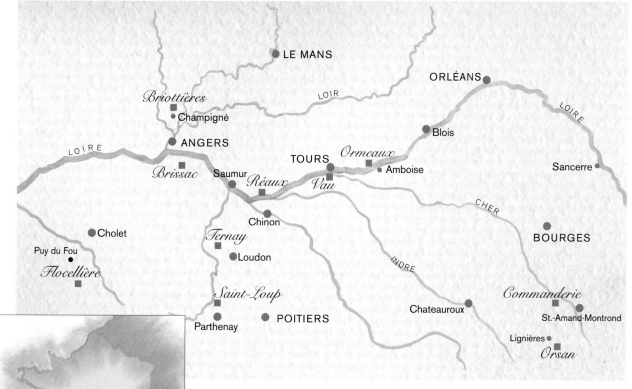

THE LOIRE IS A REGION PARTICULARLY DEAR TO MY HEART as it's been home to our family since 1992. Parisians are apt to remark on *la douceur* of the Loire Valley, and it's true that the pace of time seems to decelerate as you step off the train at a sleepy rural station here.

No one is in much of a hurry and the expression *Touraine quart d'heure* implies that locals are unlikely to show up for an appointment *à l'heure*. The civilized rhythm does engender a remarkable quality of life and an appreciation for beauty and refinement—attributes that attract visitors worldwide to marvel at the Loire's exquisite limestone châteaus, regal towns, and groomed *paysage*. Even the language is reputed to be at its purest in the Loire—here people take the time to articulate.

The exact geographic boundaries of the Loire Valley are somewhat subjective, but when Unesco classified it

PAGE 58, CLOCKWISE FROM TOP: *Loir River, north of Angers; Touraine farmhouse door; spring in "the garden of France."* OPPOSITE, CLOCKWISE FROM TOP: *Château de Brissac; château-bottled Anjou-Villages rosé; detail of seventeenth-century painted shutters; guard hall. Brissac, 15 kilometers south of Angers, is among the Loire's most imposing châteaus. Soaring to a height of 48 meters with 206 windows, 200 rooms, and 15,000 square meters of habitable floor surface, it has been the home of the Cossé-Brissac family for five hundred years. It is currently occupied by the young marquis Charles-André, his wife Larissa Szechéni (a former classical dancer with the Royal Ballet of London), and their four young children. The Queen Mum of England, Sophia Loren, and Roger Moore are among notable overnight guests, and several suites are available for just us folks at royal rates. Among the offerings are idyllic views over the manicured park, wine tastings of château bottlings, and table d'hôte dinners and receptions.*

a World Heritage Site in 2000, the riverside towns of Sully and Chalonnes were designated as the eastern and western limits. Often referred to as the Valley of Kings, the magisterial Loire region was the historic home of France's royalty and playground of its nobility. Iconic towns are strung like charms along the length of the river—Gien, Orleans, Blois, Amboise, Vouvray, Tours, and Saumur, to cite a few. Beyond the principal royal châteaus, there are over sixty castles open to visitors. I encourage you to venture beyond the best-of list to explore the dozens of lesser-known, private châteaus. These are the authentic repositories of regional patrimony—family homes filled with original furnishings, historic mementos, and idiosyncratic collections. The proprietors are pleased to regale you with recommendations for wine tasting, obscure historic monuments, and favored artisans.

There is a high standard of craftsmanship in the region. One of its treasures is the village of Vilaines-les-Rochers. Thanks to a cooperative founded in 1849, the village houses the ateliers of 80 of France's remaining 150 weavers who craft 70 percent of its osier baskets, trays, garden borders, and furniture. Faience and stoneware pottery are other traditional artisan products here. And when it comes to fine art, the combination of exceptional light and aristocratic patronage has enticed famous artists over the centuries from Jean Fouquet to Leonardo da Vinci and William Turner to capture and embellish the region's subtle beauty.

There is an eclectic range of activities for all ages and tastes to alternate with visits to historic towns and monuments. Cycling, nature tours, horseback riding, and hot air ballooning are easily organized. There are a burgeoning number of public golf courses, adventure parks, child-centric museums, zoos, animal preserves, and swimming lakes. In high season—from April through October and especially in July and August—innumerable festivals, themed town fairs, *brocantes* (flea markets), concerts, *son et lumière* displays, and dance and theatrical performances provide round-the-clock entertainment.

Garden lovers too are spoiled for choice between April and October, when a remarkable variety of parks and private gardens are open for visiting. *Parcs*

et Jardins circuit brochures are readily available at tourist centers found in most historic towns and villages. The Château of Chaumont west of Blois has a world-class Garden Conservatory that has become a horticultural laboratory for international garden designers and artists invited to create innovative themed gardens each year.

The Loire River is France's longest and was once a busy transportation artery until railways siphoned off freight traffic. It is considered the last of Europe's wild rivers and is permitted to evolve in response to its natural rhythm with a minimum of benign intervention. Its width expands and contracts as it meanders eastward, and water level fluctuates considerably with the seasons. In summer, the river is dotted with sandy islets, which testify to its limited navigability. Boating is confined to kayaks, sculls, rowboats, and the occasional single-sail *tou à voile* fishing barque. Fish are plentiful, although fishing is regulated to protect migratory species headed for spawning grounds, including salmon, shad, sea lamprey, and eel.

Its flora and fauna are diverse, and the banks of the Loire are a playground for beaver, otter, and migratory birds. The forested regions north and south of the river remain active hunting territory. Since the 1970s, when conservation measures were set in place, the wild boar, deer, and roe deer population have exploded along with buzzards and other birds of prey.

Hunting—from the sandy pine marshes of Sologne to the oak forests of Touraine—is a popular pursuit with enthusiasts from every niche of society. *Chasse à courre* (hunting with hounds), the traditional sport of kings, continues to gain followers. Passing by a forest any Saturday between October and April, you're likely to hear a huntsman's horn and the cry of the hounds or catch a glimpse of a hunter on horseback, looking like a figure from a nineteenth-century print, resplendent in velvet-trimmed redingote and stock tie.

My favorite season is spring, when the Loire Valley earns its reputation as the garden of France. *Potagers* (kitchen gardens) are a hive of activity after winter dormancy and impeccably pruned fruit trees and flowering shrubs burst into bloom. Roses thrive in the region and are at their peak May through June. Autumn is another glorious season. The foliage puts on a

OPPOSITE, FROM TOP: *Touraine limestone wine hut stained with the copper sulphate used to treat vines; wildflowers, Pontlevoy.* BELOW: *Troglodyte dwelling near Amboise.*

display of subtle nuance, and outdoor markets are stocked with harvest treasure—ripe apples, pears, amber squash, and wild mushrooms fresh from the woods.

Chèvre cheese is a regional specialty, as are all manner of fowl, river game, and pork, which is transformed into *rillons*, *rillettes*, sausages, and terrines. The quality of regional wine has become consistently good, and prices, except for the most exclusive vintages, remain affordable. There are numerous appellations and a variety to suit all tastes including Chinon, Montlouis, Vouvray, Cheverny, Bourgueil, Menetou-Salon, Sancerre, Saumur-Champigny, and Anjou.

While the Loire Valley between Orléans and Angers is celebrated for its familiar landmarks, the property selections here venture south into neighboring Berry, Poitou, and Vendée. These crossroads regions share enduring historic and cultural links with the Loire and have a dense concentration of monuments and unspoiled countryside. Appreciated by French tourists yet less frequented by foreigners, Berry, Poitou, and Vendée have preserved their rural integrity. Their visited attractions tend to be less crowded and commercialized than other Loire sites.

A rule of thumb is that popularity tends to erode authenticity. It is usually more satisfying to explore a less crowded village, château, or church where you have the freedom and tranquility to observe and set your own pace in a spot where you won't have wait to sit down for a quick meal. You are also more likely to receive a sincere welcome and have an opportunity for exchange, as your presence isn't taken for granted.

The pageantry of the Loire's noble legacy is felt at every turn. Its wealth of fabulous architecture, gilded history, and graceful countryside give it the character of a dreamscape, where fantasy and imagination are continually engaged. Though not technically located at the midpoint of the hexagon of France, the region is called the *Centre* and the Loire Valley is indisputably a jewel in the crown of French patrimony. ✺

OPPOSITE, CLOCKWISE FROM TOP: *château and village of Montrésor in the Indrois River valley; twin alleys of maple and chestnut trees, Château de Saint-Loup, Vendée; June hay harvest.*

Château des Réaux

LABOR OF LOVE

Le Château des Réaux is a lovely base from which to explore the historically rich stretch of the Loire between the cities of Tours and Angers. Villandry with its incomparable gardens, the "Sleeping Beauty" Ussé, and fortified Langeais—which hosted the wedding of Charles VIII and Anne of Brittany—are all nearby châteaus. Les Réaux's Renaissance pedigree is irreproachable—it is one of three Touraine châteaus commissioned by Jean Briçonnet, the first mayor of Tours, in the fifteenth century. Like its upstream castle sisters, Chenonceaux and Azay le Rideau, Les Réaux is the centerpiece of a romantic water setting.

The proprietors of the château are the Bouillé family. Madame de Bouillé's great-grandfather purchased Les Réaux in 1895. A distinguished Egyptologist, he added a wing on the south facade, which incorporated his exotic *cabinet* of oriental curiosities. The war years took a heavy toll, and the property lay uninhabited for fifteen years until Jean-Luc and Florence de Bouillé reclaimed the property with gusto in 1979.

The project became a loving hands-on restoration, driven by the practical skills of Monsieur and Madame's passion for her childhood home. When you meet the chic and vivacious Madame de Bouillé, it's hard to imagine her covered in plaster dust. Today you are more likely to spot her on television in her role as ambassadress for one of several historic associations.

The entry drive of Les Réaux leads to a wooden bridge spanning a ring moat irrigated by the Loire. An arched carriageway cuts though the distinctive checkerboard towers to the courtyard and park. The gardens flowing beyond are a medley of

The Bouillé Family's
COUPS DE COEUR

Candes-St-Martin

Situated at the confluence of the Loire and Vienne rivers, the twelfth-century collegial church is built on the site where Saint Martin died in 397. Visitors are treated to memorable panoramic views.

Chinon

This landmark town on the banks of the Vienne River is a fifteen-minute drive from les Réaux. The cobbled streets and medieval château (now an impressive ruin) witnessed some of the more dramatic moments in France's early history from the reign of Henri Plantagenet to Joan of Arc's legendary audience with Charles VII in 1429.

Cadre Noir, Saumur

Just west of Les Réaux, France's internationally renowned riding corps performs for the public April through September, at the national riding academy located on the outskirts of the city.

Mushroom Hunting

Fall is the prime season for mushrooming in the national forest north of Bourgueil. A fun way to explore this magnificent stretch of protected parkland north of the Loire.

Picnicking in the Gardens of Villandry

Les Réaux is a twenty-minute drive from the sumptuous Renaissance gardens and ornamental potager (kitchen garden) of this château. There is a family connection since the Bouillés' daughter, Angélique, is married to the Villandry's owner, Henri Carvallo.

*L*ike its upstream castle sisters,

Chenonceaux and Azay le Rideau,

Les Réaux is the centerpiece of a

romantic water setting.

landscaped exterior spaces reflecting important epochs in the château's history: a medieval herb garden, Renaissance *potager* (kitchen garden), eighteenth-century neoclassic follies, and nineteenth-century romance.

The latest phase was designed and planted by the owners' energetic daughter-in-law. Nicky is a native of New Zealand, who met husband Stanislas as a young professional in London. She threw herself into the project after settling at Les Réaux, as a means of integrating her new and former lives. The nineteenth-century garden plantings are informed by her mother's passion for English gardens.

Stanislas has evidently inherited the family knack for masonry. His latest feat was unearthing the remains of a Renaissance kitchen while excavating near the chapel. As "restored ruins," they became the architectural backdrop for the couple's garden and *Vinothèque* project. Thanks to their ingenuity, you needn't travel further than a charming garden *cellier* (wine cellar) and al fresco terrace to sample the best of neighboring Chinon, Bourgueil, and Saumur Champigny vintages. Nicky is also the taste maven behind a smart boutique with a stylish selection of regional decor and gift items.

Like Château des Briottières near Angers, Les Réaux is a pioneer among *châteaux d'hôtes* (château guest houses). While maintaining delightful spontaneity, the experienced Bouillé family keeps a step ahead with their fresh range of services for visitors. ✄

Château du Vau

FAMILY FARM IN TOURAINE

Four generations of the Clement family live and work at the Château et Ferme du Vau. Ninety-four-year-old Madame Clement, who was born there, has always been a proponent of moving on with the times. Given a choice between several family château properties as a young married woman, she chose Vau because of its potential as a working farm. When grandson Bruno proposed opening the house to guests, she was all for it.

The appeal of le Vau is its informal family atmosphere. Bruno and his wife Nancy thrive on contact with visitors. "We have wonderful guests," enthuses Bruno. "Big houses like Vau have a tradition of welcoming visitors, especially foreigners. Because we're self-contained, it's important to be receptive to others." Bruno is an affable host, who readily shares his passion for wine and enjoys helping guests plan their tour of the region. His outgoing personality is complemented by Nancy's gentle temperament. She's the domestic whiz, seemingly unflappable in the kitchen and discreetly pulling strings behind the scenes.

They were encouraged by the experience of his uncle Edouard, who took over management of the farm twenty years ago. Edouard and his wife Joëlle transformed a livestock operation, which was struggling to compete with international markets, into a successful foie gras business. The timing was right for Bruno and Nancy to relocate with their young children from Paris and embrace a rural lifestyle. For Bruno, the château is like an old childhood friend he's delighted to have rediscovered.

Nancy & Bruno Clement's
COUPS DE COEUR

The Château Grounds

The privacy and tranquility of the property is a privilege the Clements never take for granted. Whether strolling in the park or wandering out to explore hidden ponds and woodland, you'll find that the grounds are a continual source of discovery.

Prieuré de Saint Cosme

The poet Ronsard lived in the fifteenth-century cottage on the priory grounds and is buried in the chapel. The vast garden is a peaceful haven with over two hundred varieties of roses and iris. Nancy loves the exceptional atmosphere and glory of the gardens in spring.

Saché

Balzac and American artist Alexander Calder both found inspiration in the serenity and isolation of this sleepy village. The Château de Saché has preserved the room where Balzac wrote some of his finest novels. The Auberge du XII Siècle restaurant is highly recommended for refined country cuisine.

Château de Gizeux

This family château north of the Loire is surrounded by 1,976 acres and has a surprising fresco gallery of royal châteaus including Fontainbleau and Versailles, painted by Italian artists in the late seventeenth century.

Château de Langeais

This fortified castle is wonderfully preserved. The exceptional fifteenth-century interior contains many historic treasures, including seven tapestries (1520–1540), considered the most beautiful in the region. The château is a captivating visit for children.

Cocooned by 272 acres of pasture and woodland, Le Vau is remarkably protected for its close proximity to the city of Tours. It has the added luck of having the eighteen-hole Golf de Touraine as its closest neighbor. The combination of verdant rural setting on the outskirts of the Loire's capital city and easy access by car to the châteaus of Villandry, Saché, Azay le Rideau, and Langeais explain why visitors didn't take long to discover it.

The guest house launched modestly in 1994 with one bedroom and has gradually expanded. Two recently opened rooms in the east wing were major renovations, and

the results are elegant and impeccable. Nancy's sentimental favorite is the grandmother's former bedroom (Madame

Clement now lives in the house next door) with its suite of English maple furniture and aura of a bygone era. Brass beds, cozy sleeping alcoves, and Laura Ashley prints and wallpaper lend the overall decor a British flavor that complements the eighteenth-century architecture.

Large picture windows located in the front and back take in lovely views. "Country houses in the eighteenth century were designed as a pretext to sit and look out over the park," claims Bruno. After centuries of putting up barriers against the threat of attack, châteaus in the age of enlightenment were designed to take in the beauty of their surroundings.

For visiting families, Le Vau has the distraction of a working farm with plenty of animals to observe. A tour of the *élevage* (breeding farm), *laboratoire* (industrial kitchen), and boutique is a fascinating introduction to artisanal foie gras production. Edoaurd is a dynamic personality, always seeking to improve and expand the sophisticated product line. He is proud of their control over production of the foie gras and defends the tradition of force-feeding the animals to enrich their livers. "Because we cultivate our own organic corn, I know that the grain given to the ducks and geese is top quality. Some people don't like the *gavage* process, but the ends justify the means, which is more than you can say for politics."

Joëlle creates recipes for terrines, *confits,* and the regional specialty, *rillettes. Rillettes* are a rich pâté of shredded duck or goose meat, which has been simmered in a marmite of "healthy" duck fat. Served on crusty baguettes, *rillettes* are an aperitif staple in Touraine. Commercial varieties can be pasty, but Joëlle's *rillettes d'oies* are a melt-in-your-mouth savory delicacy. A recent addition to the line is duck sausage, which Bruno recommends for summer barbeques.

Table d'hôte dinners permit guests to sample many of the farm's specialties. In the warm summer season, the meal tends to be a casual buffet served in the garden. At cocktail hour, there's a large pool and acres of lawn for children to let off steam after a day of sightseeing, while adults can admire the delicacy of a Touraine sunset over the unbroken view of pristine countryside. 🌿

Château des Ormeaux

ON THE GENTLE SHORES OF THE LOIRE

The north bank of the Loire has always been a privileged residential location because of its elevated southern exposure. This is especially true between Tours and the royal city of Amboise, where Château des Ormeaux is cradled against the hillside with a commanding view over the river valley. The nearby village of Nazelles marks the eastern limit of the Vouvray vineyards, which spread across five neighboring valleys sloping down to the Loire. The area's microclimate favors production of the Chenin Blanc grape, which lends local Vouvray wine its tingling character.

Secluded within a 64-acre park, Les Ormeaux is on the outskirts of Amboise and a brief drive from Chaumont, Chenonceau, and many other Loire Valley landmarks. The compact, vertical château with twin hexagonal slate spires backs up to a tufa rock cliff carved out with troglodyte (cave) dwellings. These remarkable habitations are characteristic of the region and have served as shelter since humans first took up residence on the shores of the Loire. Initially quarried for the characteristic white stone used to construct châteaus and manors throughout the region, the caves subsequently were used for wine production and storage. Limestone is an excellent natural insulate that maintains a constant temperature, keeping caves agreeably cool in summer and warm in winter. The soft texture of the rock and its luminous pale color create a surprisingly agreeable ambiance. For visitors seeking a unique Touraine experience, Les Ormeaux has a cozy troglodyte guest room that looks out onto a romantic floral garden. Facing south, the interior catches and reflects light throughout the day.

Emmanuel, Eric, & Dominique's
COUPS DE COEUR

Château de Chenonceau

This iconic Renaissance castle straddling the Cher River was the domain of exceptional women. Examples include Diane de Poitiers, a king's favorite; the widowed Queen Catherine de Médecis, who confiscated it from her rival; and eighteenth-century arriviste and beauty Madame Dupin, whose literary salons are legend.

Clos-Lucé Manor and Park

Leonardo da Vinci spent the final years of his life (1516–1519) at King Francois I's childhood home in Amboise, orchestrating special events for the court. The master brought with him several favorite paintings, including the Mona Lisa (now in the Louvre). There is a fascinating installation of scale models of Leonardo's inventions created by IBM engineers.

Auberge de la Croix Blanche, Veuves

"Simply delicious" is Dominique's description of the no-frills regional menu at Jean-Claude and Emmanuelle Sichi's country inn nine miles east of Amboise towards the city of Blois.

Gardens of Château Valmer

Renowned horticulturist Alix de Saint Venant revitalized the historic gardens of the family property (which also includes a rare troglodyte chapel and Vouvray vineyard). The visited gardens feature Italianate terraced parterres, a vast ornamental potager (kitchen garden) with hundreds of unusual varieties, and a collection of flowering trees and shrubs.

L'art de vivre, or gracious living, is cultivated at Les Ormeaux. The gentle pace and refined surroundings make table d'hôte dinner both an elegant meal and a relaxing opportunity for exchange.

Sun pervades the château's elegant ground-floor drawing rooms, which overlook the broad Italianate terrace. The first hint of the house's musical theme is a grand piano in the salon. The twentieth-century composer Francis Poulenc was a resident of Nazelles, and an Art Deco guest room on the second floor is named for him.

More formal guest rooms on the first floor are themed around eighteenth-century composers. The Lully and Couperin have handsome period decor and antiques. The entire château was renovated in 1998 and the rooms with ensuite bathrooms are all well-lit and imaginatively appointed. Couples traveling together who prefer a degree of independence can opt for a charming eighteenth-century *logis* (gatehouse) adjacent to the château with two spacious guest rooms and terrace.

A jewel-like pool is tucked discreetly below the château balustrade, sheltered amid the landscaped garden. Sun worshipers will appreciate its protected southern exposure. For the energetic, walking paths cut up through the wooded hillside to the vineyard and open country beyond.

Table d'hôte dinner is a regular feature on Monday, Wednesday, and Saturday evenings. The château has its own small vineyard that produces a limited quantity of Touraine white for private consumption. One of the owners, Emmanuel Guenot, gained extensive restaurant experience working at Ledoyen and Regine in Paris and Box Tree and Trois Jean in Manhattan. It was upon his return from New York in 1998 that he and two partners purchased Les Ormeaux. Each has his particular expertise—Dominique Pepiot is the computer and operations maven, while Eric Fontbonnat has an applied language and business degree.

The three proprietors rotate responsibility for receiving and caring for guests, but everyone pitches in on the preparation of homemade jam, which is served at breakfast and sold in a boutique adjoining the kitchen. Loire Valley wines, local produce, and a selection of tableware and accessories are also available for those guests wishing to take home mementos without the hassle of a last-minute rush. 🎋

Château des Briottières

A FAMILY AFFAIR

François and Hedwige de Valbray sparked a trend when they first opened Les Briottières to guests in 1979. At the time, the concept of *chambres au château* and hosting *les étrangers* still shocked fellow *châtelaines* (château owners). Fortunately, the Valbrays were too young and enterprising to be dissuaded. While there are many imitators today, there's nothing like the original. Les Briottières continues to set a standard for excellence and authenticity in family châteaus.

The B&B bug definitely bit the family. Inspired by François's success, a younger Valbray sister and brother have both opened family châteaus to visitors in the city of Saumur and Basse Normandie. As François described the relative merits of each property, I detected a healthy touch of sibling rivalry—which no doubt encourages a high level of service. The siblings have even developed an "all in the family" circuit, with reduced rates for a stay at two or more of the family properties.

The drive to Les Briottières north from the city of Angers meanders past hedgerows, fields, and sleepy pastureland dotted with dozing cows. The pace rapidly downshifts along this bucolic stretch of farmland between the Sarthe and Mayenne Rivers. Your destination is nestled amid 50 acres of graceful parkland, a few miles past the historic Plessis Bourré castle.

The Valbrays' professionalism is a boon for pampered guests. Their home effortlessly combines the elegant refinement of a château with the comforts of home.

Château de Serrant
West of the city of Angers, the château is reknowned for its magnificent period furnishings.

The Cointreau Distillery
Located in Angers, this is a fine place to visit to experience a French classic.

Solesmes Abbey
Visitors enjoy hearing the Gregorian chants at this Benedictine monastary, which is located near the city of Sablé.

The park at Briottières
"There isn't a day I fail to appreciate the beauty and tranquility of this park," says François. "I love that we live in such a calm place yet can be in Paris within an hour and a quarter taking the TGV from Angers."

Château Langlois Saumur Blanc
François is partial to his cousin's Vielles Vigues white and sparkling Cadrilles Crémant de Loire wines.

Visitors are encouraged to decompress around the secluded pool within a walled garden, to fish by the lake in the shade of willows, or to explore the idyllic Angevin countryside on an all-terrain bike. As parents of three teens, the Valbrays are expert at keeping children amused. In addition to swimming and tennis, there is ping-pong, badminton, a trampoline, tree swings, and even a piano for distraction. Adults can also enjoy an after-dinner game of French billiards in the library with the host.

Cuisine is an essential component of *l'art de vivre* (gracious living) at Les Briottières. An exclusive partnership with Le Cordon Bleu, France's most prestigious culinary institute—with twenty-two schools in twelve countries—is a highlight of the summer season. A young Cordon Bleu chef takes up residence to perfect his or her skill in *l'art de recevoir* before donning a toque at a Michelin two-star restaurant. Many of the young chefs are foreign graduates, and Hedwige relishes the synergy of their partnership. "These young professionals are sent here to get in touch with the reality of running an establishment. I encourage them to create menus featuring local produce and combine their savoir faire with our family recipes. Living and working with us, they really learn about French culture."

At sunset, guests are invited to unwind with their hosts on the terrace over a glass of the region's golden Coteaux de Layon. It is a relaxing opportunity to share the experience of a dynamic couple whose enthusiasm for their vocation and the region is contagious. ❧

Château de Ternay

TURRETS AND TRUFFLES

Loic de Ternay has the distinction of living in a château bearing the family name, which his ancestors occupied for three centuries. Far from blasé, Loic is committed to preserving and animating Ternay, considering it a duty to transmit its history to younger generations.

The property is a hive of activity, combining the functions of family home, visited historic monument, B&B, and working farm producing truffles, nut oil, and honey. With four school-age children living at home, family comes first and guests are swept right into the rhythm of daily life.

Ternay is a captivating place for children from four to ninety-four, who are fascinated by knights, chivalry, and the pageantry of medieval and Renaissance history. Loic transformed a sprawling attic space into a heraldic workshop where he conducts seminars for school groups and vacation camps. An interactive approach incorporating games, storytelling, and handicrafts dramatizes the history, architecture, and daily life in and around Ternay (which played a pivotal role at the conclusion of the Hundred Years War). Another child-friendly attraction is the warren of limestone tunnels beneath the site of the former medieval fortress—a veritable troglodyte (cave) village that once housed a community of feudal artisans.

In the nineteenth century, the keep and moat were eliminated to create a more pleasing residential château, but there is no disguising Ternay's fortified origin. The fifteenth-century construction is architecture of transition. The château was

90

Caroline & Loïc de Ternay's
COUPS DE COEUR

Cuisine de la Truffe Weekends
During truffle season, from mid December through February, Ternay hosts weekends themed around this versatile gastronomic treasure. Guests join Loïc in the truffière and discover the infinite ways truffles can give recipes distinction.

Château de Montsoreau
Formerly a thriving Loire port, Montsoreau was the ancient frontier between the provinces of Touraine and Anjou. Today it is classed among France's most beautiful villages, and the gleaming fifteenth-century limestone château on the water's edge houses an imaginative installation, Les Imaginaires de Loire, which traces the history and legend of the château and its river.

Architectural Distinction of Ternay's Facade
The variety of openings, crenellations, and stonework make the château viewed from its exterior a singular visual treat.

Château de Brézé and souterrains
Surrounded by vineyards, this refined Renaissance château has the deepest dry moat in Europe (18 meters). It sits atop an underground fortress with nearly a mile of tunnels housing caves (storage cellars), distilleries, wine presses, and a four à pain (bread oven).

Sharing Family Heritage
Even if at times it is a burden, the Ternays respect the importance of maintaining and sharing their home as a living monument.

built as the Hundred Years War was ending, and military criteria had diminished. The clearest expression of this duality of style is the Gothic chapel built within the fortress walls. While camouflaged from the exterior, the elaborately sculpted facade punctuated with windows dominates the inner courtyard. A Protestant lord built the chapel as a gift for his Catholic wife. (The city of Loudun was a long-standing Protestant stronghold.) The intimate sanctuary is on the second floor. Of particular note is a rare and well-preserved seventeenth-century folk art crucifix encrusted with miniature sculpted instruments of Christ's passion. It is thought to come from the region of Brittany and is known as a "Stations of the Cross" crucifix. Another treasure is a 1470 carved wood pietà from Burgundy.

The decor of the residential wings at Ternay retains a nineteenth-century aura. The salon has some fine seventeenth-century paintings inset on panels above the doorways and Aubusson tapestries adorning the walls. A magisterial stone staircase leads off the salon up to nostalgically furnished guest rooms.

Ternay really comes to life midwinter during truffle season. The Loudun region was an important truffle market in the eighteenth century, and Loïc's father revived the tradition fifteen years ago. The region's climate is favorable, as the ground rarely freezes solid. Truffles thrive around the roots of certain varieties of green oak and hazelnut trees. A circular patch around

the trunk of a tree called *la brulée* indicates the target zone of *mycorizé* soil harboring tubers. Rather than use pigs, which must be muzzled to discourage them from ingesting the prize tubers, Loic works with dogs in his *truffière*. Since dogs don't find truffles delectable, they are trained to forage for them with cotton imbibed with truffle oil. When they scratch the ground to indicate a find, their keen sense of smell is rewarded with a handout of bacon. Ternay's unlikely truffle-hunting champion is Okase (slang for secondhand), a mutt that doesn't even bark and was rescued from a dog shelter. Loic attributes her truffle detection skill to an eager-to-please temperament. "Okase is so attached to us, she loves the work. Calm, homebody dogs seem best suited for the job."

Loic's wife Caroline especially enjoys this season because guests may more fully partake of country life. As family chef, her most rewarding season in the kitchen is when the pungent aroma of the black melanosporum tuber is at its peak. Fresh truffles are a luxury partly because of their limited shelf life. (Top grade can fetch up to $1,300 per kilo.) After a week they must either be frozen or preserved. Because cooking diminishes flavor, they are typically used raw to retain the distinctive *craquant de la truffe*. Family-style table d'hote meals in the château's spacious country kitchen become a celebration of thriving tradition.

Château de la Flocellière

"FLOWER OF THE SKIES"

Guests at La Flocellière are immersed in a millennium of history. A reward of straying from the habitual tourist trail is that one encounters such unexpected treasures as châteaus that were once important fiefs and bore witness to the wars, passions, and political intrigues of France's turbulent past. For those seeking a historic home experience, this enchanting estate is hard to beat.

First cited in 1090, La Flocellière became a principal fortress of the ancient province of Bas-Poitou by the Middle Ages. Its architecture (extensively restored in the nineteenth century) is a graceful composite of thirteenth- through seventeenth-century construction, tracing the evolution from military to residential style. Six towers of varying epochs, romantic ruins, and stately gardens with a profusion of flowers conspire to charm visitors within minutes of arrival. A bird's-eye view from the balustrade of the terrace garden over the *Haute Bocage*—rolling farmland crisscrossed by hedges and trees—suggests why the château gained its feminine name "flower of the skies."

Vicomte Patrice Vignial has an encyclopedic knowledge of his property's legacy and vital role in the region. His attachment is doubly personal since La Flocellière had been in his family prior to the French Revolution. In 1979, Vignial had the satisfaction of purchasing the château back after it had passed through several owners, and he and his wife dedicated themselves to preserving and enhancing its exceptional character over the ensuing quarter century.

Erika & Patrice Vignial's
COUPS DE COEUR

Table d'Hôte Dinners
Erika loves setting a beautiful table and sharing a quintessential country meal. The exchange is always fascinating and allows guests to fully partake of la vie à la française.

La Rochelle
The coastal city of La Rochelle is eighty minutes away. It is a lovely maritime destination with museums, historic sites, and four ports. A bridge connects the mainland to the chic resort of l'Isle de Ré.

Domaine du Closel
Unesco nominated the Savennières vineyard landscape a World Heritage Site. The Closel château appellation produces white Savennières and Anjou reds. Tastings and tours of the Jessy Pontbriand seventeenth-century family château and vineyards are available.

Château de Terre Neuve
This is the private renaissance château at nearby Fontenay-le-Comte, where writer Georges Simenon resided during World War II. It is famed for its rare alchemist's fireplace and carved stone ceilings, wood paneling from Chambord, and superb seventeenth- and eighteenth-century costumes.

Locals
As somewhat of an outsider herself, Erika is impressed by the friendly, welcoming character of the Vendée region. After a career in Paris it was a delight to discover how agreeable it is to work with local personnel.

The Vicomtesse, Erika Vignial, a Swiss native and former director of public relations for cosmetics giant l'Oreal, is ideally qualified to manage and promote a luxury product. She has compiled a trove of information on the region, which opens the door of discovery for guests. Suggested itineraries are meticulously mapped out—from a tour of the nearby Savennières wineries, to a visit to the magnificent Château Serrant with its historical interiors, to a day at neighboring Puy de Fou. At this historic park, two thousand years of French history from the gladiators

on are brought to life through dramatic reenactments and reconstructed period environments across 99 acres of parkland. This ambitious project is a new attraction in the region and one the Vignials enthusiastically recommend. It is one of the most exciting venues of its kind in Europe and provides marvelous entertainment for both adults and children.

The Vignials' daughter, who subsequently moved with her young family to Switzerland, initiated the B&B activity ten years ago. Erika took over and surprised herself with how much she enjoys it. Accustomed to the pace of Paris and frequent travel, she was initially apprehensive, but the challenge of diversifying and expanding their services keeps it stimulating. Among her preferred activities is organizing costumed Renaissance evenings. Erika takes care of renting elaborate costumes, which await guests in their rooms. A chef specializing in authentic period menus prepares the meal, and diners are serenaded by live Renaissance music. The vicomte and vicomtesse preside and frequently invite friends to join the party, for a royal night of entertainment.

Erika also enjoys the role of long-distance wedding planner. Her reputation for sophistication and organization has increased the demand for her services, but she remains selective. Ensuring each event is unique requires considerable investment of her time. "I enjoy anticipating the taste and demands of clients and surprising them with something that surpasses their expectations."

The château's interior is elegant without being intimidating or stuffy. A glimpse of the salon conjures up visions of *mondain* (society) house parties and evenings sipping cognac in front of the fire. There's an effortless chic about the place that puts one at ease and makes guests pleased to be a part of it all. Dinner in the formal *salle à manger* (dining room) on heirloom porcelain, silver, and crystal is a highlight of your stay. The Vignials are aesthetes who cultivate the beauty of their surroundings and are happy to share the pleasure with visitors. They frequently join guests at table d'hote meals, although young children are encouraged to dine separately. For special occasions, a gastronomic menu cooked by a one-star Michelin chef may be arranged.

Guest rooms are exceptionally refined. Their fine antique furnishings perfectly enhance the historic character of the setting. A romantic touch is working fireplaces set with an artful arrangement of firewood. Awakened by birdsong, with a view from the tower overlooking a renaissance well and a trellis of roses in the garden below, you really can be princess or prince for a day. 🌿

Château de Saint-Loup

LIAISONS DANGEREUSES

"I've been ruined by a ruin," laments proprietor Charles-Henri de Bartillat, with the roguish laugh that punctuates his dry irony. He jests about this magnificent Poitou landmark like a man who can't bear to break off relations with a high-maintenance mistress. In Bartillat's case it was love at first sight when he discovered Saint-Loup in 1981. He is a man with a taste for fast cars and high-risk stakes, and the château's dilapidated state simply fanned his ardor. "I should have been an architect for *Les Monuments Historiques*; I'm such an uncompromising purist that I can't concede to restoring something less than perfectly." Bartillat finally gained possession after a decade of wrangling and red tape, since the property had been donated to a charity that ultimately couldn't afford to maintain it.

The estate has played a central role in the history of Poitou. After the Battle of Poitiers in 1356, the Black Prince imprisoned French king John the Good in the former fortress. A symbolic hearse recalls the event over the entry to the Renaissance keep. The moat is a vestige of the fortified château, whose high walls once encompassed the village. Louis Gouffier—reputed to be the Marquis de Carabas who inspired Perrault's tale of *Puss In Boots*—built the existing château between 1609 and 1626, on the ruins of the fortress. It is of the same epoch as the Place des Vosges in Paris, and the facade was originally painted with similar trompe-l'oeil brickwork. To honor Henri IV, the architect designed the building in the form of an "H" composed of two large end wings and a central pavilion. Each segment of the

Charles-Henri de Bartillat's
COUPS DE COEUR

Hotel de Cygne Restaurant

A five-minute drive from Saint-Loup, the former chef of the Closerie de Lilas in Paris has set up his own modest restaurant serving country fare.

Abbey of Fontevraud

This is one of France's premiere monastic complexes. Eleanor of Aquitaine, queen of France and England, is buried there, along with several Plantagenet monarchs who reigned over Anjou.

Thouet River Valley

Enjoy the unspoiled countryside flanking this Loire River tributary by following the hiking path south from Saint-Loup to the village of Gourgé.

Parthenay

This sleepy provincial town, due south of Saint-Loup, has sustained its medieval spirit. Preserved ramparts, churches, and narrow winding streets set the mood.

Saumur

Charles-Henri encourages visitors to experience the beauty of the Loire around Saumur, to visit the royal château, immortalized in the illuminated Très Riches Heures of the Duke of Berry, and to wander the streets savoring the ambiance of the most Balzacian Loire city.

construction has an independent roof, which adds visual interest, and the central wing is topped with a decorative campanile.

While the château is exceptional, it is Bartillat's project of returning the grounds to their former glory that has returned Saint-Loup to the spotlight. The ambitious plan to resuscitate the eighteenth-century orangerie and adjacent walled gardens captured the imagination of the Ministry of Culture, which helped underwrite the project with public funds. The design is a re-creation of original 1745 plans, and the faithful restoration is astonishing. Visitors are transported to another era when

strolling through the regal enclosure with its symmetrical harmony of miniature orange trees and flowering topiaries in uniform planters.

The orange trees spend half the year adorning the formal garden, then are moved inside the orangerie from late October until *les saints glaces* of May 11, 12, or 13, when the risk of frost is over. It is a huge production, which was complicated during the first year when restoration fell behind and the fragile trees had to be shipped back to Corsica for winter storage. This experience was preferable to the year they were brought out early to accommodate a wedding and were felled by a frosty night. Ever the purist, Bartillat points out the unusual pattern of the orangerie's brickwork floor. To support the immense weight of lead planters, bricks were laid sideways to double their density.

Pruning of the trees respects a strict 3/3 formula whereby the depth of the boxy planter, height of the fine trunk, and clipped ball of fruit and foliage each comprise one third of the total height. As was customary in the eighteenth century, citrus trees are alternated with flowering trees trained into topiary cones along the manicured paths. The fragrant medley of jasmine, honeysuckle, and orange is exquisite.

Eleven guest rooms and two suites have been refurbished between a wing of the château and the fifteenth-century keep. Gazing out the mullioned windows of a Gothic bedroom in the tower, guests are treated to a postcard view of château, gardens, and verdant countryside.

The château's ground-floor interiors are traditional reception rooms, used principally for parties and special events. However, guest rooms are grandiose, appointed with canopied beds, antique furnishings, and comfortable seating arrangements. Saint-Loup is a dream destination for a romantic getaway. To complete the fantasy, couples may arrange for a candlelit dinner in the canal pavilion with its enchanting view up the length of the tree-lined waterway. 🦋

Prieuré d'Orsan

HARMONY BY DESIGN

Monastic medieval gardens were inspired by biblical imagery. Their beauty was a projection of paradise, intended to remind the devoted of the reward awaiting them for a life of good works and prayer. In 1995, two architects and a master gardener set about re-creating paradise on earth at the twelfth-century Prieuré d'Orsan in rural Berry, the mysterious *pays* south of the city of Bourges, where folklore inspired the novels of George Sand and superstition pervades.

The old priory was in ruins when Sonia Lessot and Patrice Taravella took it on without a specific project in mind. Tara, as Patrice prefers to be called, described their goal as finding a significant property to restore, then allowing the place to reveal itself and inspire a concept.

The idea for medieval gardens came during the first hot summer spent shoring up ruins, when Sonia and Tara were in want of a shade tree in the deserted central courtyard. Neighbors came by with documentation on the former priory, where legend has it the heart of Robert d'Arbrissel, twelfth-century founder of the Fontevriste order (based at the Abbey of Fontevraud), is buried. Surprisingly, Fontevriste monasteries were reserved for women, many of whom were aristocratic wives banished by husbands needing a convenient way to replace them with another woman. In a nod to local lore, the gardener trims the climbing ivy in the shape of a heart.

Sonia and Tara are architects, not botanists, and reasoned that landscaping should be based on similar principles. Tara

Sonia Lessot & Patrice Taravella's
Coups de Coeur

Live Poultry Market at Saint Août

As the cock crows Tuesday mornings, buyers, sellers, and yawners gather on the road between the towns of Lignières and la Châtre amidst a cacophony of beating wings and cackling fowl of every description. Catch this traditional rural exchange before EU regulation renders it extinct.

L'Assemblée du Plaix Folk Festival

The two-day festival takes place at a little moat-encircled château each third weekend of August in Saint-Hilaire-en-Lignières. Bonfires illuminate evening festivities, animated by bag-pipers and folk dancers in traditional costumes.

Church of Saint Genès at Châteaumeillant

Stillness pervades this twelfth-century Romanesque monument. Of particular note is the harmonious beauty of capitals carved with stylized leaves, animals, and gargoyles.

Roses in Flower at Pépinière des Pigeats

The perfume exuded across acres of rose bushes in flower at Marie France and Jean François Sarrault's nursery is hypnotic. The fields are hidden to discourage theft but are a must destination for rose lovers.

La Fromagerie des Étangs

At this goat cheese producer in the village of Ardenais, visitors may pet the goats and sample ripe little crottins (goat cheese)—delicious with a glass of Pascal Desroches's Reuilly Gris.

philosophically describes their landscaping theory as "a concept where plants are at the service of the garden design like bricks in a building. We wanted something that would be interesting year round, utilitarian more than decorative, where beauty is the end, not the means."

With the guidance of *paysagiste* (landscaper) Gilles Guillot, they transformed Orsan into an intimate enclosed garden using characteristic elements found in illuminated medieval manuscripts. The dozen garden spaces radiating out from a central stone fountain include a hornbeam cloister, rose arbor,

medicinal-herb garden, kitchen garden labyrinth, and trained fruit tree orchard. The grounds, open to the public, are considered among France's exceptional private gardens. Orsan is the subject of several books and is especially renowned for its elaborate woven willow and chestnut trellises, benches, and barriers.

Because the garden is a destination at some remove from tourist centers, La Table d'Orsan restaurant quickly followed. The seasonal cuisine has a Mediterranean predilection for allowing the flavor of fresh produce to predominate over elaborate sauces. Organic produce comes direct from the garden or is sourced from small local suppliers. Tara, the chef, applies his architectural principles to the menu—ingredients are selected to follow a theme such as red and green, sweet and sour, or contrasting play of texture.

La Maison d'Orsan guest house opened in 2002 in the former monks' dormitories and refectory. The decor is streamlined and soothing. A restrained palette is warmed by pine paneling, rosy exposed stone, plump cushions, and billowing bedcovers. An ingenious feature is the ground-floor cloakroom stocked with anything visitors might need to enjoy exploration of the garden: widebrimmed straw hats, rubber gardening clogs, umbrellas, walking sticks, and a complete shoe-polishing kit.

The serenity pervading the house and gardens is akin to that of a retreat center or spa. Prieuré d'Orsan really approaches paradise when contemplation combines with apprenticeship on a gardening or cooking workshop weekend. Gardening devotees can perfect the art of pruning and planting under Gilles Gullot's expert guidance. For the culinary crowd, Tara conducts cooking weekends customized to the size and skill of the group. 🌿

Château de la Commanderie

LA DOLCE VITA

The Berry region is defined more by state of mind than geographic boundaries. As with most of France's traditional *pays*, which existed long before bureaucrats divided the country into modern departments, inclusion is determined by subjective, "know it when you see it" criteria. To say that rural Berry is the heart of the hexagon is literally and figuratively correct, and Château de la Commanderie has been at this epicenter since the eleventh century. The village of Farges Allichamps is a convenient distance from the north-south chain of highways that intersects the country from Calais on the English Channel to Montpelier on the shores of the Mediterranean—a fitting coordinate for a château that welcomes visitors with all its heart.

Guests are immediately put at ease by co-proprietor Laura Ronsisvale's laughing eyes and spontaneous warmth. Umberto and Laura Ronsisvale embody the best of European hospitality: Italian by birth, Spanish by ancestry, and Francophile to the core. They acquired La Commanderie in 2002 from the Jouffroy-Gonsans, an aristocratic family who had owned it since the seventeenth century. The Ronsisvales were captivated by the château's domestic charm and are determined to preserve the ambiance of a family home.

Umberto, an international lawyer, has lived and worked throughout Europe, as well as in China and the United States, while Laura, a Bologna native, was a police officer in her former life. The couple discovered French *château d'hôte* (château guest house) hospitality as tourists and were impressed by how much friendlier they are than comparable villa bed-

Laura & Umberto Ronsisvale's
COUPS DE COEUR

Aprement Floral Park
In the midst of a medieval village on the banks of the Allier River, the complex of gardens is continuously in flower from April through September. Laura admires the plays of contrast and is partial to the white garden, inspired by Sissinghurst in England.

Sharing Their Home
The Ronsisvales' emotional generosity is expressed in Laura's sincere admission, "I love the fact that people feel truly at home here."

Noirlac Abbey
A national historic monument, the Cistercian abbey built in 1150 has been impeccably restored by the state. The eight sacred and residential elements of the complex are remarkably well preserved and the architectural purity of the interiors makes it a reservoir of peace.

Six-Hundred-Year-Old Oak
Like the château, the venerable tree visible from the rear terrace has witnessed scores of generations come and go.

Immersion in Nature
Umberto, who spends part of every month traveling to cities for his profession, delights in the sensory pleasure of returning to the countryside. Being in touch with the cycle of the seasons in the countryside is deeply satisfying.

and-breakfasts in Italy. To preserve the experience of staying with a family, they prefer to limit bookings to four rooms. They also removed road signs to discourage drop-ins. The reduced traffic enables the Ronsisvales to share meals with their guests and get to know them. Umberto admits, "We're doing this because we love it, not as a business. We enjoy the exchange between people of different cultures. Our guests are treated like friends, not clients."

The château was built for the commander of the Templar knights, an order of monk-soldiers who fought in the Crusades. It was then a hospital for the

Knights of Malta, until it became a residence of the counts of Jouffroy-Gonsans. The Ronsisvales are consequently

only the second family to own the estate in three hundred years.

In 1998, the gardens were opened to the public. Laura admits it is less manicured since reverting to a private enclave because they have focused energy and resources on restoring the château. Set apart from the landscaped park surrounding the château, it is quite the secret garden with its profusion of roses and perennials. Bordered by a canal with a picturesque bridge, it has a dreamy romantic character that is a refreshing antidote to the rigid formality of many château gardens. There is a lovely oasis of water lilies shaded beneath weeping willows near the old *séchoir* (drying shed). The Ronsisvales have plans to reconfigure the planting, and Laura hopes to construct a greenhouse for orchids.

In the nineteenth century, a manor house wing was grafted onto the imposing circular tower of the château. The house's human scale, ivy-covered walls, and entry porticos make it particularly inviting. This is the wing where Laura, Umberto, and their teenage son have settled. The entry hall connects both buildings and there is a natural to-and-fro between them. The eight guest rooms are divided between the two, allowing a choice between country manor and classic château ambiance.

The reception rooms on the first floor of the castle are wonderful for parties. There is a grand piano in the salon and a convivial ambiance. Smaller dinners take place in the family dining room on the ground floor. The excellent chef has a restaurant in the area that is open only on weekends, which allows him the flexibility to concentrate on both clienteles. The menus he creates with Laura showcase local produce, favoring imaginative preparation over tired classics.

A novel amenity on the property is a heliport, which connects La Commanderie to Paris in an hour. It is an especially useful connection in July when Formula 1 enthusiasts come over for the French Grand Prix races in Magny, just 46 miles away. Umberto, a confessed enthusiast, is the first to head for the races in his vintage Rolls Royce. ❦

DORDOGNE & AQUITAINE

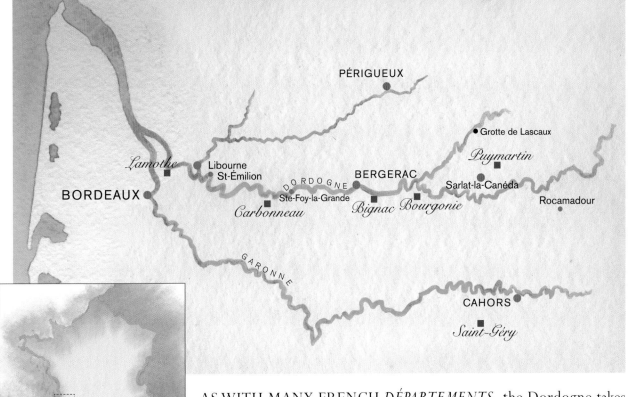

AS WITH MANY FRENCH *DÉPARTEMENTS*, the Dordogne takes its name from a celebrated river. Property selections for this region are concentrated along the legendary Dordogne Valley, which cuts across the lower third of what was historically known as the province of Périgord.

The journey begins farther south, with a stop in Quercy, a *pays* bridging the Midi and Périgord, to satisfy amateurs of full-bodied Cahors vintages and hearty southwestern cuisine. We then travel west along the Dordogne river valley through mythic Périgord Noir with its show-stopping succession of cliff-top châteaus, and west into Gironde.

Dordogne and Gironde are departments of the Aquitaine region—internationally renowned for its vineyards and wealth of gourmet produce. The six featured properties skirt several of France's best-loved food and wine

destinations, including Sarlat, Bergerac, Saint-Émilion, and Bordeaux. The Dordogne department encompasses 2.5 million acres centered around the city of Périgueux. Because the natural landscape is so varied, it is divided into four color-coded geographical segments. Green Périgord in the north around Nontron is known for its dense forests of oak, beech, and spruce trees. White Périgord is the central region around Périgueux—so called because of its vast limestone plateau. Purple Périgord in the southwest around Bergerac is wine country and the gateway to the Bordeaux region. Périgord Noir is the gastronomic heart of Dordogne—deriving its name from the somber foliage of native green oaks. Its capital is the medieval city of Sarlat.

Clement weather and abundant natural resources have attracted settlement to Dordogne since the awakening of civilization, as evidenced by innumerable prehistoric sites—the most famous of which are the Lascaux caves with their ancient wall paintings.

Second to Paris, Dordogne has the richest legacy of historic monuments in France. Beyond prehistoric grottos, there are over fifteen hundred châteaus and manors, troglodyte (cave) dwellings, four hundred Roman churches, and storybook *bastide* towns with fortified castles nestled in the hills. Garden lovers will be enchanted with Dordogne's gardens, including award-winning Marqueyssac, featuring thousands of intricately trimmed boxwoods, and the *domaines* of Eyrignac and Cadiot.

Famed for its dramatic river valleys, verdant landscape, and magnificent forests, the region is popular with nature lovers. Dordogne is an angler's paradise and a mecca for cyclists, kayakers, hikers, and equestrians. For the less ambitious, it's an idyllic setting for leisurely promenading, riverside picnicking, or escaping into books you've longed to attack.

Festival season runs from the beginning of July through the end of October. Although summer is dynamic, autumn is the quintessential Dordogne season, when morning mists lend a fairylike aura to the timeless landscape. Winter is a moodier time—the season to seek refuge behind thick stone walls in front of a crackling fire.

The holiday markets in Sarlat are the most authentic this time of year. Périgord truffles are ogled like precious jewels in *marchés*, where a kilo of "extra" black melanosporum truffles can fetch 1,100 euros. Foie gras, *confit de canard*, and *magret* are among the gastronomic treats the French indulge in on special occasions. No *réveillon* (Christmas and New Year's Eve) celebration is complete without foie gras accompanied by a honey-toned *vin moelleux*. Walnuts are the humble star of Périgord cusine. Since 2001 they have been honored with an official appellation label that distinguishes four varieties, the most prized of which are the Grandjean and Franquette. The walnut is integral to regional cuisine and is showcased in flavored vinegars, oils, liqueurs, preserves, and a host of baked and preserved delicacies.

The Dordogne Valley west of Sarlat segues into wine country. Bergerac is one of France's best-kept secrets with thirteen appellations. It is also the host of a lively music festival in July. Saint-Émilion is a medieval site worthy of discovery even without the draw of its hallowed vineyards. The tour ends at the cusp of the Dordogne Valley and Bordelais around Libourne.

Dordogne and Aquitaine are destinations for *flâneurs*—havens of meandering medieval villages, markets for sampling gastronomic delicacies, noble vineyards, and sleepy cafés. Henry Miller claimed that Dordogne comes closest to paradise of any place on earth. He might just be right. ❧

PAGE 118, CLOCKWISE FROM TOP: *village of Urval, Dordogne; Aquitaine vineyards; monolithic troglodyte church, Saint-Émilion.* PAGE 120, FROM TOP: *medieval town of Saint-Émilion; Quercy Blanc windmill.* PAGE 121, CLOCKWISE FROM TOP: *traditional Dordogne lauzes stone roof construction, Beynac-et-Cazenac; cases of foie gras, Domaine de Saint-Géry; village garden, Urval.* PAGE 122, FROM LEFT: *autumn potager crop; Beynac-et-Cazenac, overlooking the Dordogne River.* BELOW: *outdoor market, Sarlat-la-Canéda.*

Le Domaine de Saint-Géry

IN PURSUIT OF PERFECTION

Proprietor Patrick Duler is a culinary Don Quixote in quest of the perfect foie gras. He may have achieved it with his organic *escalopes* and terrines ennobled with "black diamond" truffles, but the restless Patrick is ever tasting, testing, and traveling. Saint Géry is open to visitors only four months a year, from May until September, because the serious business of foie gras doesn't reward dilettantes. The Dulers prefer to go direct to their clients, which necessitates traveling back and forth to gastronomic fairs through the fall and winter months.

The family farm is transformed into a luxury B&B late spring though early fall—a period of relative calm following fall-winter foie gras promotion and truffle harvest. *Chambre d'hôte* season coincides with summer vacation for the family's two boys, when horses are grazing in the pasture and the heated pool comes out of hibernation. It's also when Patrick reclaims his chef's apron in the farmhouse kitchen.

The *domaine* was purchased by Patrick's father as a sentimental gift for his stepmother, a member of the St-Géry clan. The ruined hamlet had been the farm for a château dismantled during the French Revolution. While a student in Toulouse, Patrick couldn't spend enough time there. He loved the singularity of the place and the fabulous climate. Though technically within the *Département* of Lot, Quercy Blanc, southwest of Cahors, is culturally and gastronomi cally linked with the Dordogne Valley region. It gets its name from the chalky earth and white native stone. Historically a poor region of modest farmers tending vines, fruit trees, and flocks of sheep, its undulating plateau is fissured with a network of small rivers and dotted with windmills.

Pascale & Patrick Duler's
COUPS DE COEUR

The Well of Aujols
In this Lot Valley village in the Causses de Quercy fourteen feuding families dug wells sixteen feet apart, tapped into the same source.

Faïencerie Duran
Pascale has many requests for the source of her beautiful faience tableware. The town of Martres Tolosane, 37 miles south of Toulouse off the A64-E80 highway, has remained the faïence capital of southwest France for three centuries.

Didier Soligon, Artisan Ironsmith
A regional craftsman, Solignon sculpts and forges both functional and decorative pieces. The Dulers have commissioned several of his imaginative creations.

Église de Lachapelle
This recently restored eighteenth-century Baroque chapel looks remarkably like an Italian theater. Several theatrical performances are put on every year.

Twenty-Five-Acre *Truffière*
For its unique ambiance, timeless magic, and panoramic view of the undulating Quercy landscape beyond the trees, Patrick appreciates his truffle oak plantation. Its discreet character demands a subtle eye to interpret its signals.

The Duler gastronomic adventure was launched in the late 1980s with an ad hoc weekend restaurant with open chimney and three tables. Business was drummed up by distributing flyers on car windshields. Word of mouth drew a loyal clientele intrigued by Patrick's spontaneous approach to cooking. Primarily an autodidact, he continues to augment intuition and experimentation with intermittent cooking workshops with leading chefs.

His biggest break was Pascale, who showed up to inquire about catering a party for her family and never left. The husband-and-wife team has since transformed a weed-choked hamlet into a thriving family enterprise. Patrick's seductive bravura complemented by Pascale's fragile sophistication is a winning combination.

Their ancient farmhouse is a classic Quercy construction in blocky white stone. The front entrance and reception rooms are on the first floor. A flight of steps leads to the traditional covered terrace (*bolet*), running the length of the house. The ground floor is reserved for cellars in this wine-making region.

The farmhouse's central room is the hub where guests are greeted with an open fireplace. This is the Duler home, where meals are served either on the covered porch overlooking the rolling countryside and village beyond, or at fireside. Patrick prepares succulent *magret de canard de Barbarie* steaks on the open fire and serves them with woodsy wild mushrooms and a favorite Cahors, such as Château Lagrézette or Clos Triguendina. Lascabanes is a few minutes' drive from the Cahors vineyards and, not surprisingly, Patrick is as demanding about what he drinks as what he eats.

The menu is meat-centric but vegetables are handled with comparable flair. Specialties include foie gras *mi-cuit* with pink peppercorns; *porc noir Gascon* (black Gascon pork—which tastes nothing like any pork you've experienced); and hand-cut foie gras and magret sausage flavored with Armagnac brandy. Pascale is the aesthete who sets a gorgeous table replete with embroidered linens and customized faience.

Guests enjoy plenty of privacy. Rooms are spread among various

restored buildings within the hamlet. Each room is well appointed, and most have a private terrace with pastoral view.

An exercise facility and all-terrain bikes are at your disposal plus miles of hiking trails cleared in the woods. Horse riders can accompany Patrick on an equestrian tour of the 148-acre property, where he is keen to show off the expanding *truffières*. Truffle production in the region fell into decline after World War I when farm widows didn't have time to tend the green oak plantations. Once the plantations became overgrown and sun deprived, productivity died off. The replanting of new trees began in the 1980s and there has been a veritable renaissance since. A truffle oak takes ten to fifteen years to mature, so harvest levels build slowly. The Dulers are gradually expanding their plantation on farmland and expect truffles to develop into more than an ingredient for meat specialties.

The Dulers take advantage of spring to travel and compare their hospitality with foreign experiences. Pascale finds it keeps them on their toes, saying, "It gives us balance since living in the country you're in danger of getting cut off." Luckily for visitors, complacency doesn't come with the territory. ✖

Le Château de Puymartin

THE WHITE LADY OF BLACK PÉRIGORD

The Dordogne Valley rivals the Loire for concentration of remarkable châteaus, although their character is distinctly different. Throughout the Périgord region, the Hundred Years War between England and France was followed by a century of religious conflict. Prolonged civil strife left its mark on the region's architecture, and Dordogne châteaus conjure visions of heavily armored knights flashing swords and torrents of fiery arrows arching over crenellated battlements. The fortified châteaus tend to be set on defensively chosen promontories, and their ochre stone walls capped by massive *lauze* (stone-flagged) roofs convey impenetrable solidity.

Dominating the Beune Valley in Périgord Noir, the Château de Puymartin is the quintessential Dordogne forteresse. Centrally located between the city of Sarlat and prehistoric Les Eyzies on the "route of a thousand and one châteaus," it could be the prototype for a Lego castle with all the extras. The photogenic eastern flank, which undoubtedly dripped boiling oil on the heads of enemies, is not the entry angle. Co-proprietor Countess de Montbron, whose husband's family has resided here since 1450, is partial to roses and would prefer visitors' first impression to be the fragile blooms of her lovingly tended *massifs* (flower beds).

Because Puymartin has remained the property of the same line of aristocrats for centuries, it is an important repository of family and cultural history. The Montbrons opened their home to the public in 1972, "because we got tired

Xavier de Montbron's
COUPS DE COEUR

The Suspended Gardens of Marqueyssac

Spectacular views of surrounding châteaus compete for your attention with the boxwood garden where 150,000 bushes are hand-clipped into an astounding variety of organic forms. On Thursday nights during July and August, paths are illuminated by candles till midnight.

Ameublement Rouchon, Sarlat

This is Xavier's sister Bernadette's boutique. She specializes in furniture and decorative objects for the home and has decorated many regional hotels and private homes.

Château de Fénelon

A feudal fortress in the countryside between the towns of Sarlat and Souillac, it is a hybrid of medieval and Renaissance architecture from the fourteenth to the seventeenth centuries. Birthplace of the celebrated Fénelon, an influential cleric, academician, and bureaucrat, it also features collections of arms and armature.

Château de Commarque

This dramatic ruined twelfth-to-fourteenth-century keep and fortified village has a remarkable view of the Beune Valley. Abandoned in the seventeenth century due to dilapidation, since 1968 it has been revived by descendant Hubert de Commarque, who is conducting ongoing excavation and restoration.

Cinema Rex, Sarlat

A valuable cultural asset for cinéphiles, with a program of nondubbed foreign films and classics, it organizes a four-day festival the first week of November, bringing together professionals and aspiring film students.

of turning the curious away," claims Xavier. Among its treasures are important Aubusson and Flemish tapestries, Louis XIII table and chairs, Louis XV desk, Regency commode, and numerous paintings.

Their pièce de résistance is a curious mythological cabinet painted in 1651 in grisaille (a mixture of egg white, charcoal, and pigment). The intimate chamber—designated a historic monument—was the creation of a visiting artist for nobleman Antonie de la Pluyie, who had a fascination with Greek mythology and is said to have contemplated its mysteries before making important decisions. The scenes make

allegorical references to political events of the day—a period following *La Fronde*, a failed coup by powerful nobles against Louis XIV at the start of his reign. Nineteenth-century prudery took a toll when certain figures were painted over with strategic drapery. Other rooms retain seventeenth-century decorative painting over fireplaces and on coffered ceilings.

The château's two *chambres d'hôte* opened in 1985 and, as Xavier explains, "were really an excuse to refurbish some nice guest rooms for friends who come to stay." The larger of the two had been the suite of the former Countess de Montbron, who passed on Puymartin to her youngest son Henri in 1982. It is a lovely sunny room, which was completely renovated in the 1920s, and its spacious bathroom, while updated, retains some wonderful fixtures from the era. The second guest room on the main floor has two enormous his-and-hers neo-Gothic four-poster beds. Both rooms have comfortable sitting areas and enough personal trinkets to convey the impression that you happen to be a houseguest of the family.

If you've contemplated the thrill of spending a night in an authentic haunted property, this is your chance. The tragic *Dame Blanche* (White Lady) is said to wander the castle to compensate for years of confinement under house arrest. Puymartin was a Catholic stronghold when Protestants

held Sarlat during the religious wars, and the jealous seigneur suspected his wife, Thérèse de Saint-Clar, of infidelity with a Protestant. Her lonely cell adjacent to the guardroom in the watchtower became a tomb when she was interred in the wall at her death. Count Henri sighted the melancholy spirit on several occasions.

Breakfast is served either in the *salle basse* (lower salon), surveyed by a collection of ancestral portraits, or on the adjoining central terrace, cheerfully appointed with flowering plants. The countess and her eldest son Xavier, who recently assumed his late father's duties, are delighted to share recommendations for preferred restaurants in Sarlat. Madame is a native of Sarlat and can suggest how best to explore the town and environs. A daughter with a busy decorating business in Sarlat has restored a home on the grounds, and a second son has a family agricultural property in the region, so the family remains well anchored in their former fiefdom—an original destination for immersion in French provincial aristocracy, with a soupçon of eccentricity.

Château de la Bourgonie

NOBLESSE OBLIGE

Hubert and Christine de Commarque have not one but three château properties in the Dordogne Valley *and* the most venerable family name in the region. The most celebrated of the properties, yet quite uninhabitable, is Château de Commarque, a Byronesque ruin of a feudal fortress that was abandoned in the seventeenth century and reclaimed in 1968 by Hubert, who has made its restoration his life's work.

The Commarque family residence is Château de la Bourgonie, a distinguished *demeure* constructed in the fourteenth and seventeenth centuries around a large central courtyard on a manicured 74-acre estate of gardens, pastures, and woodland. The third property, La Poujade, is a short drive east in the hamlet of Urval—one of the most picturesque settings in the Dordogne Valley. The classic U-shaped *chartreuse* (rural residence)—the largest in Périgord—is the sentimental favorite since it returned to the family through a felicitous marriage in the early part of the century and was a historic resistance headquarters in World War II. This sleeping beauty, which accommodates fifteen, is available as an independent weekly rental.

Christine and Hubert have the endearing quality of being thoroughly blue-blood yet spontaneously warmhearted and solicitous of guests' comfort—a reminder of why the definition of snob is *sans noblesse* (lacking gentility). Our world may not be theirs but they are delighted to make their world ours for a night or two. Scrapbooks attest to the lure of

L'Esplanade Restaurant, Domme

This is a family-run restaurant on the heights of this landmark town with an unbeatable view of the Dordogne River Valley.

Château de Commarque

An extraordinary setting for the repository of 80,000 years of human history, the château holds a sculpted horse head discovered in the caves that is a masterpiece of prehistoric culture.

Independent Garage and Regional Train Station, Le Buisson

At a time when gas pumps and small-town train stations that are there when you need them are a dying breed of rural service, the Commarques appreciate how useful they are for visitors.

Chapelle de Notre-Dame, Temniac

A Romanesque chapel on a hill north of Sarlat is a pilgrimage site every September for veneration of its black virgin.

Yvon Charpenet, Ironsmith

Hubert admires this talented artisan who produces beautiful customized designs for his clients as well as utilitarian objects. He constructed a lovely garden gazebo for La Bourgonie.

Jean Lacombe, Foie Gras Producer

A local farmer who respects the land and continues to be dedicated to a traditional lifestyle which he exercises with great integrity, Lacombe produces some of the best local foie gras.

An enormous trellaced grapevine on the terrace at La Poujade is reputed to be the largest and oldest in Dordogne.

the place, including homage by writer Julien Green. The couple met through an environmental association thirty-two years ago and remain committed crusaders for the natural world. They stick to organic produce, and the new swimming pool has a salt-water filtration system. Hubert heads an association for the protection of microdevelopment in the region and is thrilled that after long bureaucratic battles, he succeeded in having Château Commarque's remote valley designated a protected zone.

Commarque isn't the sole ruin Hubert has rescued from the brink. La Bourgonie was relegated to cows when he rediscovered it when camping out for his elder brother's wedding, which took place at a Commarque family château in Urval. He recognized its greatness despite the mud up to the windowsills, and convinced his mother to back up the project.

Hubert lost his father at an early age. As wartime mayor of Urval, Gerard de Commarque was denounced for falsifying identity papers and deported to the Nazi Buchenwald concentration camp. Their mother never remarried, and Hubert grew up in relative isolation with an English grandmother, the former Miss Greenwell, whose father purchased La Poujade in 1900. His grandmother took the risk of allowing La Poujade to house the general quarters for the coordinated French and English resistance in the southwest. Coincidentally, the chartreuse was also a secret depot for treasures removed from the Louvre and Luxembourg Palace for safekeeping. André Malraux, the novelist who became Charles de Gaulle's influential culture minister, was among those installed at La Poujade at war's end. In 1982, the family organized a reunion for the Anglo-French officers, who completed the unfinished business of draining the family wine cellar.

Having two not-quite-independent children based in Paris helps the Commarques keep a foot in the present. Hubert is hopeful that his son Jean will have the will to sustain his struggle to preserve Commarque. The site is an ongoing archaeological dig. Having been abandoned since the 1600s with no consequent development, it is unusually well preserved, and work undertaken is primarily clearing and reinforcement. A rare castrum

(fortified habitation) and grottos with significant prehistoric artwork have already been uncovered. Hubert is particularly thankful for private support for medieval research from American foundations such as the Florence Gould and the Getty, which recognize its enormous historical significance.

Throughout winter, the B&B is reduced to two guest rooms adjoining the family wing, and minimum stay is two nights, but from Easter through All Saints, the entire south wing is available. There are six guest rooms that accommodate eleven, independent reception rooms, and a well-equipped kitchen, which allows the option of renting the wing as a self-catering unit. It opens onto a private garden and has separate entrances to afford visitors optimum privacy. The elegant guest rooms are decorated with family antiques and tasteful fabrics. Understated refinement prevails, but comfort hasn't been overlooked and ground-floor bathrooms are fully updated.

One of La Bourgonie's best assets is its location. A train station serves the town of Buisson, and the prehistoric sites of Vézère Valley and principal Dordogne Valley châteaus are close by. A visit to the hamlet of Urval is recommended for sampling the charm of its twelfth-century church, medieval *four banal* (communal oven), and sensitively restored homes and cottage gardens clustered around the banks of the river. It is a transcendent interlude when you wish the dream wouldn't end. ✄

Chartreuse du Bignac

RETREAT FOR THE SENSES

A *chartreuse* is possibly the most agreeable residential building style in the lexicon of French architecture. Neither château, manor, nor *gentilhommière*, it manages to combine the best elements of each. Chartreuses were built as rural residences when the architectural evolution of the *maison de plaisance* (vacation home) neared completion. Its genesis corresponded with a long period of domestic peace after 1650, which held until the French Revolution. A chartreuse is a sober, rather solid structure, distinguished by classical proportions, horizontal lines, and emphasis on light and comfort.

The mayor of Bergerac under Louis XIII built Le Bignac as a *demeure de champs* (country residence) on château foundations dating from the twelfth century. Bergerac was a strategic port and bridge gateway on the Dordogne River and was Périgord's principal city prior to the French Revolution. Its mayor, appointed by the king, held a prestigious post. Like all *rural bourgeois* he valued land, even if he didn't intend to work it, and Bignac's elevation provided a panoramic view of his holdings. Three church spires are visible at various points on the horizon. Today, the property encompasses 30 acres, including a plum orchard whose harvest is dried to produce the delicious regional dried *pruneaux d'Agen*.

The current proprietors, Jean Louis and Brigitte Viargues, have restored Bignac with impeccable style and respect for the integrity of the original design. The couple decided to embark on a joint project when they wound down careers in Paris, and they confined the quest for an inspiring property to the southwest since Jean Louis is a native and Bergerac is appealingly situated at the crossroads of Périgord and Aquitaine. The village of Saint Nexan is a ten-minute drive

Brigitte & Jean-Louis Viargues's
COUPS DE COEUR

Jardins of Cadiot

This private oasis covers 5 acres with gardens themed by color and motif. They include the poetic, the English, the savage, the boxwood, the labyrinth, and the peony, with more than one thousand varieties in continual flower. An art exhibit of African sculpture by established and emerging artists is integrated into the landscape.

Le Cloître, Maison des Vins

A former cloister of the Recollect order and landmark of the reestablishment of Catholicism in Bergerac at the close of the Wars of Religion, Le Cloître is now a cultural center showcasing the rich history of the wines of Bergerac, as well as a host to concerts and exhibitions.

François Pastry & Chocolate Shop

After a walking tour of Bergerac, this is the place to stop and indulge in one of François's marvelous pastries or heavenly homemade ice creams.

Point d'Orge Boutique

If you need a thank-you gift for the person walking your dog or minding your kids, this stylish Bergerac boutique has a well-stocked selection of decorative, household, and wedding gifts.

Château Binassat

Owned by the same family for over 150 years, this wine estate specializes in sweet wine. Their latest creation, Pepite, is made from 60 percent muscadelle, and imparts remarkable fullness and suppleness. Their red and white wines have won prizes at the prestigious Mâcon fair.

Brigitte's decorating style combines romanticism and modernity with a touch of whimsy. The effect is stunning and every room is a fresh encounter with subtle harmonies in fabric and furnishing.

from an airport served by domestic and budget airlines, which allows Jean Louis to commute to Paris when needed for consulting work.

The extensive restoration took two years, and they opened their home in 2002 with eight guest rooms. Brigitte's decorating style combines romanticism and modernity with a touch of whimsy. The effect is stunning, and every room is a fresh encounter with subtle harmonies in fabric and furnishing. Guest quarters are a feast of comfort and visual stimulation. Every aspect of comfort has been provided for. The bathrooms are virtual mini spas, with jewel-bright towels and fun but functional decorative accessories.

The Viargues are oenophiles and gourmets, and they quickly made friends among the local producers. The location in the heart of the Dordogne wine region is an endless source of discovery for them. One glance at the cathedral ceiling kitchen at Bignac confirms you are in gastronomic territory. *L'art de table*—as with every component of *art de vivre*—at Bignac is *recherché,* and dinner served before the fire in the intimate dining room is a romantic treat. A local cook assists Brigitte and the resulting menu is a satisfying update of traditional regional cuisine. The jewel in the crown of regional appellations is golden Monbazillac, a sublime accompaniment to local foie gras. Guests are encouraged to enjoy an after-dinner liqueur in the salon, where a sizable

humidor is a nod to Bergerac's status as the French capital of tobacco.

The rear terrace overlooks a large, landscaped pond frequented by local ducks. In fall, morning mist tenderly blankets the landscape, giving way to gentle sunshine. Recreational features include a sleek pool and a home theater, where guests can screen a classic of French cinema while enjoying a glass of hearty Bergerac rouge or aged Pécharment.

The Viargues are two executives in transition to a slower tempo, recognizing perspective gained from a change of scenery. They have organized several executive retreats at Bignac. A second dining room is discreetly equipped to be transformed into a contemporary conference center when the need arises, and there are plenty of excursion opportunities and sporting activities to enliven downtime.

The ambiance at Bignac is a hybrid of two cosmopolitan spirits: Jean Louis's intellectual aura and Brigitte's sensory sophistication. If the timing is right, a visit may coincide with a concert or art exhibition. As with an increasing number of rural regions, there is a high concentration of international and ex-urban residents around Bergerac, particularly in summer. The Viargues believe a like-minded audience exists for cultural events in a private setting, and there are few more idyllic spots in which to stage one. ✖

Château de Carbonneau

W I N E   A N D   H O S P I T A L I T Y

The history of Château de Carbonneau is serendipitously linked with that of New Zealand. Both were created 150 years ago, and over the ensuing years, three generations of women born in New Zealand have made the château their home. Co-proprietor Wilfrid Franc de Ferrière's mother, a New Zealander by birth, moved to France at twelve when her Franco-Russian parents acquired the property in 1930 to pursue dairy farming. A family fondness for cows persists and Wilfrid raises a wooly herd of Aquitaine Blonde beef cattle when not pursing the more glamorous activity as *viticulteur* of fine Bordeaux wines.

Built during the fin de siècle wine boom years, Carbonneau retains a fashionable feature of this era, an ornate Napoleon III greenhouse. Carbonneau's original owner was both a gardening enthusiast and Americanophile. His legacy to the château's park is several outstanding North American specimen trees, including a giant sequoia and a magnificent magnolia.

The vineyards became a casualty of the 1929 financial crisis, and wine production ceased until Wilfrid revived the château appellation after inheriting the property in 1992. He currently produces eighty thousand bottles of AOC Sainte-Foy Bordeaux from 32 acres of vines planted on surrounding hillsides. The wine *chai* (building for aging wine) is contiguous with the house, and Wilfrid adheres to traditional vinification techniques, with 20 percent of production aged in oak barrels and the rest in stainless steel *cuves* (tanks). The wines are elaborated from Merlot, Cabernet Franc,

Jacquie & Wilfrid Franc de Ferrière's
COUPS DE COEUR

Le Château de Duras
The château's history spans the twelfth through the eighteenth century. Jacquie recommends the self-guided tour, saying, "There is plenty of scope for the imagination," with thirty-five restored rooms, an ethnological museum, an armory forge, and a program of historical dramatizations.

Moulin à Eau de Moustelat
This restored eighteenth-century watermill was owned by the Grand Master of the Wine Brotherhood of Sainte Foy-Bordeaux. Owners Béatrice and Robert are pleased to conduct guided visits that include an old working four à pain (bread oven) and a tasting of the wines produced on their 32 acres of vines.

Castelmoron d'Abret
Reputed to be the tiniest commune in France, this village of narrow pedestrian passages retains the lost charm of l'autre fois (olden days).

Market at Sainte-Foy-la-Grande
Saturday morning is the prime time to explore the bastide (fortified) town with its timbered houses and arcaded halle (covered market).

Gardens of Sardy
This escapist romantic garden with Italian and English influences features reflecting pools, cypress trees, and hundreds of varieties of flowers and plants. The tearoom serves lunch on the terrace in summer, and wine produced on the property is for sale in the boutique.

and Cabernet Sauvignon grapes and exported throughout the world. This year he expanded the range with a rosé and planted some vines for white wine, which they plan to bottle in 2007. A tasting room was recently opened, but you may also visit the cellar, where glasses may be filled directly from oak barrels.

Wilfrid sets a high standard and is pleased his wine is faring well with the panel that awards coveted AOC appellations each spring. Building a brand in this competitive region demands increasing professionalism, and failure to match standards relegates even château label vintages to table wine status.

Jacquie was a schoolteacher in her native New Zealand and met Wilfrid while she was vacationing with mutual friends in the region. They married in New Zealand and settled there briefly prior to taking over Carbonneau. The Franc de Ferrières have four school-age children and Jacquie breeds Bernese mountain dogs, so days at Carbonneau are full.

The B&B activity seemed a natural extension of their lifestyle, and they welcome the international exchange it engenders. The guest wing has been extensively renovated and is accessed by an independent entrance. There is a comfortable sitting room on the ground floor adjacent to a formal dining room, where table d'hôte dinner is served in cool weather. The plant-filled greenhouse is favored for candlelit dinners in summer, and the rear terrace overlooking the park is a lovely spot for breakfast.

The ambiance at Carbonneau is refreshingly informal although there is nothing casual about the way Jacquie and Wilfrid run their household and business. Jacquie conveys Mary Poppins spit-spot efficiency and guest rooms are *tiré à quatre épingles* (neat as a pin).

Their professionalism earned them a "2005 Best Of" award this year for wine and hospitality from the Great Wine Capitals Global Network. Jacquie is a keen amateur chef, and her table d'hôte dinners prepared with *produits du terroir* (regional delicacies) are delightful.

Carbonneau's 124-acre estate is spread across a terrain of hills and valleys ideal for scenic walks. There is a secluded pool in a walled garden where a stone pigeon roost has become the pool house. Children will find plenty of distractions, including practicing baseball with the Ferrières' eldest son Hugo, a member of the French junior national team. The neighboring town of Pineuilh stages an annual tournament and in 2005, to celebrate the national team's twentieth anniversary, teams will convene from the United States, Canada, and throughout Europe. The Sainte-Foy region is evidently fertile ground for cross-cultural exchange. 🗡

Château Lamothe

LINENS AND LACE

Midway between Saint-Émilion and Bordeaux, Château Lamothe is an authentic rarity in a region crowded with "wine label châteaus" laying dubious claim to the title. Aquitaine has the highest concentration of châteaus in France, with a majority, like restoration aristocrats, a product of mercantile maneuvering. A fortified castle existed here from the eleventh century, and by the fourteenth, when the English conquered Aquitaine, Lamothe became a favored hunting retreat of its governor, the "Black Prince" of Wales. Augmenting its feudal pedigree, Lamothe is one of two regional châteaus with an *eaux vive* (spring-fed) moat, which protects its rippling waters from stagnation and creates an attractive refuge for migratory birds.

Lamothe's landholdings were drastically reduced when the state reclaimed it during the Revolution and its history as a great hunting property ended. The house was transformed from a fortress to a residence in the eighteenth century, followed by an epoch of Bordeaux wine production in the nineteenth. During this prosperous period Lamothe was restyled in the fashionable neo-Gothic Villet-le-Duc manner, and its award-winning Bordeaux *supérieure* was exported with a label reading "Best French Claret For Breakfast" (proof that the French red wine dietary benefit has been pitched for a century). The estate's belle epoque concluded with World War I, and the current owners, the Bastides, acquired the faded beauty in 1977. The family has labored to both revive its luster and protect the site, which was threatened by

The Bastide Family's
COUPS DE COEUR

Saint-Émilion

Famed for its wine, the ancient town is a symphony in ochre stone and one of only two French cities with Romanesque fortifications. The buried church excavated in the early 1900s is a marvel. The town sits atop 173 acres of subterranean galleries carved out of the limestone bedrock.

Le Grand Théâtre, Bordeaux

An eighteenth-century masterpiece designed by Victor Louis with sweeping neoclassic colonnaded facade, this is the only European theater of its epoch not to have been destroyed by fire. Period seats have been restored and performances are occasionally illuminated by candlelight.

Diane Casteja, Glass Artist

Inspired by shells and other natural forms, her work is also exhibited in Paris and at her Basque atelier. Her off-kilter champagne flutes are magical.

Château Quercy—
Grand Cru, Saint-Émilion

Enjoy an excellent visit with a producer who is generous with his savoir faire, Stéphane Aplebaum.

Native Caviar

The Garonne is the only river in continental Europe that produces sturgeon. Once a local delicacy, sturgeon was overfished, leading to a ban in the early eighties, but now fish are finally returning to cleaned-up waters, and the Moulin de la Cassadote breeding farm in Biganos on the Arcachon Basin has been the biggest producer since 1983.

encroaching development. Their happiest achievement is a protected site designation awarded by the Monuments of France architect, which prohibits further subdivision or development on the perimeter.

Lamothe is graced by a feminine touch. The Bastide women, who out-number Monsieur Bastide, influence the tone and temperature of the house. Beautiful linen and porcelain are a cult here, and Madame Bastide imports special starch to ensure that intricately embroidered heirlooms are pressed to perfection. Each guest room has examples of Luce's collection of vintage lacework, tucking, eyelet, and organdy.

Véronique has succeeded her mother as principal hostess but the Bastide seniors—who opened their home to guests in 1996 after the four daughters moved on—are still present. Other daughters live close by, so grandchildren are likely to pass through for *grand-mère*'s *pain au chocolat* fresh from the oven. The spacious kitchen is the family *pièce à vivre*. A massive eighteenth-century carving table with expandable joints for permitting juice to drain is the centerpiece of an active hearth. The open fireplace is used to prepare a regional specialty—meat grilled over *sarments de vignes*. The bundles of pruned vines are fast burning and give meat a distinctive Bordelais flavor.

Jacques Bastide, a retired *homme d'affaires*, is the grandson of a Bordeaux vintner and owned his own vineyard. He is a passionate oenophile and justifiably proud of the château cellar, where the vaults are filled with a careful selection of Bordeaux and other notable appellations. Jacques enjoys conducting tastings for guests, treating them as occasions to take out his antique decanters, glasses, and silver *tasses de vin*—a domed saucer that permits the taster to clearly judge a wine's *robe* (color). He is also pleased to steer visitors to producers whose wine offers good value, and might be persuaded to sell a few bottles from his stock if you are time pressed.

The mild, temperate climate, influenced by proximity to the Atlantic, makes Lamothe a pleasant destination well into the fall, when temperatures

in late October can feel like spring. The villages of St-Sulpice-et-Cameyrac, south of the Dordogne River at a crossroads between the Dordogne Valley and Bordelais, are situated strategically for exploring Bordeaux and its environs.

The enclosed 52-acre park is a verdant oasis with a surprising concentration of wildlife. Roe deer graze amid the trees and in fall, *coulemelle* mushrooms are harvested for savory omelets. The drive is lined with scores of rose bushes, and a devoted gardener keeps everything carefully tended. Autumn is a prime season in the garden, when roses are still in bloom, the lawn is carpeted with delicate white and mauve cyclamens, and Virginia creeper turns the château facade fiery red. Two expansive front and back terraces catch the sun at every hour. The west terrace is best for an evening aperitif, with the broad moat creating the pleasant illusion of being on an island.

Much attention is expended on the romantic decor of the guest rooms, each with a distinct personality. "We introduce guests into our life rather than transform our life to accommodate them," is how Véronique defines their philosophy. Bathrooms were installed in existing spaces rather than remodel interior architecture, and have idiosyncratic charm. Their ample proportions allow several to be furnished as boudoir sitting rooms. A first-floor salon was converted into a sunny blue-hued suite, with French windows opening onto a balcony overhanging the moat, eighteenth-century frescoes, and a divan.

Breakfast is a feast for the eye and palate. Each day the dining-room table is set with different porcelain and a coordinated bouquet. Decadently thick homemade hot chocolate is a house specialty worthy of indulgence. Guests should profit from Véronique's astonishing erudition and exhaustive knowledge of the region. She is as effusive lauding the architectural harmony of Bordeaux as she is partial to Saint-Émilion's medieval heritage. You'll leave wondering why this remarkable woman hasn't written her own guidebook. ✖

ROVENCE

EVEN IF YOU'VE YET TO VISIT FRANCE, you've likely heard of Provence. It's the region that symbolizes rural France at its most bucolic. The name evokes a tapestry of images—ancient *bastides* (fortified towns) improbably perched atop ochre cliffs, acres of lavender, Roman amphitheaters, the shimmering Mediterranean, wild Camargue horses galloping across marshland, silvery olive trees, and spires of cypress silhouetted against azure skies.

For the French, Provence is synonymous with carefree summer days, fresh herbs, wildflowers, and cheerful Provençal print fabrics that dress al fresco tables and are an enduring staple of summer wardrobes. It's a destination that puts them immediately in a holiday frame of mind.

The weather is unbeatable year round, with three hundred days of sunshine. The loveliest seasons are spring and fall, when daytime temperatures are pleasant and vegetation is at its peak. July and August, the

PAGE 162, FROM LEFT: *in the shade of a plane tree, Pernes-les-Fontaines; selection of natural regional products, Maison du Moulin.*
BELOW: *olives, rosé, and lavender are synonymous with summer in Provence.*
OPPOSITE, CLOCKWISE FROM TOP LEFT: *farm fresh eggs; church, le Barroux; homemade spice cookies, Ruiz market; the vast plateau of Valensole, near the Gorges du Verdon; herb garden, Château de Saint-Maximin; Provençal townhouse; September in the vineyards.*

traditional *grandes vacances* period, is the most animated time of the year. It's the season when backcountry villages stage innumerable festivals and starry nights are endless.

In autumn, the light is incomparable and the tempo delightful after the bustle of the high season. Winter can be blustery if the mistral blows, but crystalline skies are a welcome antidote to the gray of Paris in December.

Its unique light has made Provence a perennial artist's colony. Raking sunshine alternately intensifies and eclipses the vibrancy of the landscape. Ochre tones surround: There are the cliffs of Rousillon—where russet pigments are extracted to tint walls, fabric, and pottery glazes—rolling fields of sunflowers everywhere, and sunsets gilding the Alpilles as a backdrop. But above all, every shade of blue is omnipresent—sky, sea, lavender, rippling pools, cotton awnings, and wooden shutters screening the midday heat.

Intersected by two major rivers and bordered by the Mediterranean, Provence has been a prime destination since the time of the Roman Empire. A visit to any village or town is an encounter with history. From the remote Alpes de Haute Provence—which inspired the novels of Jean Giono, France's great chronicler of rural life—to the polyglot port city of Marseille, you'll discover monuments of antiquity, Romanesque churches, abbeys, *bastides*, and castles. Vestiges of another important era, elegant seventeenth- and eighteenth-century *hôtels particuliers* (mansions) and fountains grace the squares of many towns. Throughout the region, indigenous culture and folklore are celebrated in museums large and intimate, in countless festivals, and in boutiques showcasing world-renowned crafts and produce.

In selecting *maison d'hôtes* for Provence, I tended to skirt the coastline in favor of the less touristy *arrière-pays*. Several properties are clustered around Papal Avignon, where the Rhône and Durance Rivers intersect. This is perhaps the cultural heart of Provence, where the prestigious international theater festival is staged each summer and antique dealers are clustered at L'Isle-sur-la-Sorgue.

Provence is a region of intense hues and temperament. Its distinctive

regional accent, full-bodied red wines, and flavorful Mediterranean cuisine are expressions of this singularity. There's a boldness and verve to the natives, which complements the rugged terrain and explains why bullfighters and cowboys are the local heroes.

While states in America and counties in England tend to have defined borders with correspondingly distinct identities, France's political and economic subdivision into departments and regions isn't consistently aligned with traditional cultural boundaries. This makes it tricky to define Provence's borders. Where one guidebook includes Uzès and the Pont du Gard but excludes the Verdon Canyon region of the Alpes de Haute Provence, another cites the Rhône River as its western boundary. Not being a purist, I strove for a cross-section of beautiful landscape—including the Camargue, Mont Ventoux, Vaucluse, Luberon, and Verdon Regional Park.

There is a relative scarcity of residential châteaus in Provence compared with other regions and a preponderance of seasonal versus primary residences. Consequently the number of private historic home B&Bs managed by families who've owned them for generations is limited. However, featured proprietors who've settled there from other areas are infatuated with Provence and tirelessly uncover its secrets.

On a practical note, the new TGV Mediterranean rail link from Charles de Gaulle airport and Paris has cut travel time to less than three hours—with stops at Avignon, Aix en Provence, and Marseille. There are also regional airports in Avignon, Marseille, Montpelier, and Nice serviced by domestic and low-cost airlines with connections to major European cities.

Few regions in France can match Provence for the warmth of its beneficent sunshine, ochre-hued architecture, Mediterranean gastronomy, and meridional attitude. Its earthy exoticism and timeless mystery seldom fail to stimulate the senses and ignite a delightful feeling of *joie de vivre*. 🗡

OPPOSITE, CLOCKWISE FROM TOP: *château and hill town of Grignan, where Madame de Sévigné visited her daughter the Countess and addressed her seventeenth-century correspondence; Mont Ventoux on the horizon; one of forty fountains in Pernes-les-Fontaines.* BELOW: *view into the interior courtyard of Chateau d'Esparron.*

La Maison du Moulin

SAVORING SIMPLE PLEASURES

La Maison du Moulin, or Mill House, is nestled in the Berre river valley just beyond the historic village of Grignan, with its remarkable château cresting the hillside. Exiting onto a rocky lane off the main road, you meander down past hidden vineyards and groves of truffle oaks to a shady refuge of dappled sun and whispering willows.

At a cool remove from the heat of the plain, Bénédicte and Philippe Appels have created a cheerful haven, which artfully integrates family life with their two young daughters and their passion for promoting the best of the Drôme's regional products. The Appels are well attuned to the requirements of visitors because they, too, fell in love with Provence as vacationers. After exploring the region each summer, they decided in 2000 to swap an urban life as corporate professionals for the challenge of building a project together.

While the Drôme is less touristy than the Vaucluse region, infrastructure projects like the TGV have attracted a consistent influx of outsiders who've settled in. Bénédicte commends the generous welcome they received from locals. "Unlike Avignon and the Luberon, the Drôme region is unusually receptive to newcomers. Foreigners are well integrated in the community here."

Because renovations were undertaken with a plan for guest rooms, the comfort and privacy of guests was a prime consideration. Each room has a private entrance and a charming view. Bénédicte's decorating talent is evident, from the refinement of the guest rooms to the flair with which she styles a dinner table. An existing pool, judged too close

Bénédicte & Philippe Appels's
COUPS DE COEUR

Le-Poet-Laval—*Village Perché*

This sensitively restored medieval hill town is classed as one of France's 100 Most Beautiful Villages. Not a souvenir shop in sight!

Nyons *Marché*

Among local markets, this one on Thursday morning is a winner. Nyons is famed for its black tanche olives, exceptional oil, truffles, and lavender.

Le Vieux Moulin—
Olive Oil Press

This traditional mill run by Alain Farnoux is one of the last truly artisanal cold press facilities. In addition to his own production, Farnoux presses limited-production custom olive oil for a loyal clientele who bring their harvest from as far as Italy.

Domaine de Montine—
Côte du Rhône and Coteaux
du Tricastin Vintages

For more than thirty years the Monteillet brothers have developed a fine selection of regional wines. Married to sisters, they conduct a family business with personalized service.

Painted Clay *Santons*—
Robert Canut

Folkloric Christmas crèche figurines are a popular souvenir item, and Robert Canut is among the finest craftsmen of this regional art form. Bénédicte describes Canut as a local treasure and a "santon himself."

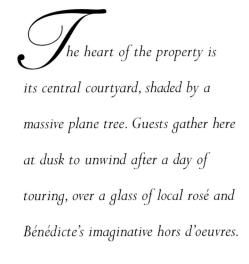

The heart of the property is its central courtyard, shaded by a massive plane tree. Guests gather here at dusk to unwind after a day of touring, over a glass of local rosé and Bénédicte's imaginative hors d'oeuvres.

to the house, was filled in and was replaced with a minimalist beauty at a quiet distance up the hillside, overlooking fields of lavender.

A neighboring farmer helped the Appels plant their truffle oaks and acres of lavender. For the Appels, perpetuating the cultivation of indigenous produce is a priority. In summer, they are a featured stop on the Routes de Lavande tour. From November through March, the Appels organize truffle culinary weekends, when the fragrant tuber is ripe for harvesting.

The heart of the property is its central courtyard, shaded by a massive plane tree. Guests gather here at dusk to unwind after a day of touring, over a glass of local rosé and Bénédicte's imaginative hors d'oeuvres—shirred eggs with truffles—and a cool melon soup piquant with the aroma of lavender. A spacious cloistered veranda serves as an outdoor dining room for table d'hote dinners in fine weather. Philippe keeps the stone fireplace stoked against evening chill.

The Appels have created an idyllic retreat, where Provençal rusticity melds seamlessly with contemporary sophistication. 🦋

L'Aube Safran

REFLOWERING OF A TRADITION

Living in Paris, Marie and François Pillet devoted their time off from work as a chef and an architect, respectively, to wine tastings and haute cuisine courses. Purists with a passion for quality and integrity, they lamented the decline of traditional methods and dreamed of owning a vineyard where they could produce organic wine. In 1993, they relocated to Carpentras and enrolled in a winemaking academy, while scouting for a few acres of vines.

It didn't take long to realize that "buying" in is nearly impossible for outsiders. In the rugged hills of *la Provence cachée*, Parisians are dismissed as foreigners synonymous with change. The Pillets' next line of attack was to research forgotten crops of the Vaucluse. At regional wine tastings, they detected distinct saffron tones and investigated. Eureka! Saffron was an integral ingredient of Mediterranean cuisine and an indigenous crop from the fourteenth through the nineteenth centuries, but cultivation had died out after World War I.

Learning that grapes and saffron thrive in the same well-drained soil conditions, the Pillets settled on a former apricot nursery in the mountains of Dentelles of Montmirail and set about planting 60,000 imported crocus *sativus* bulbs on the terraced slopes. Unlike most flowers, growing season for the saffron crocus is late autumn, when the delicate purple blooms spring up like mushrooms on the hillside. Harvesting takes place during the month of October and must be done manually, as is subsequent conditioning and packaging. It's a job that requires patience and dexterity.

The exclusive crop is lovingly packaged for retail sale in delicate glass vials, which showcase the tender russet stamens.

Marie & François Pillet's
COUPS DE COEUR

Terres de Solence—
Organic Wines

François affectionately describes the owners of the vineyards, Anne-Marie and Jean-Luc Isnard, as "winemakers with heads in the stars." Their Cuvée Cippres merits a Guide Hachette heart.

Le Batteur Restaurant

The Pillets' favorite table is in one of the region's best-loved villages. Chef Alain-Jean Artaud is never self-satisfied and is especially appreciated by discerning locals.

Jean Claude Engrand, Artist

A Grenoble native this painter of contemporary landscapes has an atelier in le Barroux. The Pillets have exhibited his work and admire his colorful and emotive abstractions of Provence countryside.

Xavier Vignon,
Consultant Winemaker

A consultant winemaker and master blender for Moët et Chandon, Vignon advises numerous estates on viticulture and vinification. Having the status of merchant à négociant, he may produce elegant assemblages (blends) under his own label, culled from some of the region's best harvests.

La Rove—Goat Cheese

This local chèvre frais (fresh goat cheese) with a unique herbal flavor of Provence is available at Josiane and Christian Deal's excellent cheese shop in Vaison-la-Romaine.

The vials are corked and tied to elegant ochre cards with a stylish crimson raffia bow. The presentation resembles prestige fragrance packaging—fitting for this sophisticated spice with its subtle yet piquant character. Saffron shares affinities with the vanilla bean but lends itself equally well to savory and sweet dishes.

It didn't take long for France's top chefs to come calling. Le Safran du Ventoux is becoming a featured ingredient on prestigious Michelin star menus. Celebrity chef Pierre Gagnaire of Lyon plans dishes around fresh deliveries, and Patricia Wells

dedicated two pages to the Pillets' achievement in *The Provence Cookbook*.

Having reconnected with *la terre* and invested their ingenuity in the cultivation of a rare crop, the Pillets focused on transforming their hilltop *mas* (farmhouse) into a stylish guest house. Francois's training as an architect and Marie's taste for harmony and natural materials have created a warm yet streamlined interior.

Because L'Aube Safran receives guests year-round, great attention was paid to cold weather comfort, with fireplaces and a golden palette. The decor of the five guest rooms was created *à l'ancienne*. Surfaces are tinted with natural pigments in subtle plays of taupe, cream, and clay, with highlights of Roussillon red and tender blue. Spacious walk-in showers are finished in satiny Moroccan tadelack, an effect created by polishing multiple layers of pigmented plaster to a glowing finish with a flat stone. Decorative objects from Maghreb and the Near East are reminders of the geographic provenance of saffron and historic links across the Mediterranean.

The *mas* has a commanding view of the peaks of Montmirail and is embraced by a garden planted with *native senteurs* (herbs)—lavender, rosemary, and thyme amid rock garden blooms. The shrubby vegetation and view at sunset through the tall pines suggest both northern California and Tuscany.

François designed a handsome invisible-border pool, which integrates harmoniously into the landscape. Natural shade is provided by olive and apricot trees, green oaks, and native pine.

Table d'hôte dinners initiate guests into the culinary versatility of saffron. Marie is a spontaneous chef who enjoys inventing and updating traditional Mediterranean dishes to incorporate her enigmatic floral spice. Terrine of monkfish drizzled with green olive and basil pesto is complemented by a crunchy *galette* of saffrony spelt. Dried stamens, infused for an hour like tea, lend subtle flavor to ice cream for Marie's delectable *Vacherin* with strawberries dessert.

True enthusiasts are invited to assist with the October harvest, which falls between September *vendanges* (grape harvest) and winter truffle season. Two hundred thousand blossoms are hand culled and the stamens dried before an open fire. The Pillets are magnets for like-minded champions of integrity in regional food and wine. They are collaborating with notable oenologist Xavier Vignon and they co-host discovery weekends around wine, truffles, and saffron. L'Aube Safran merits its reputation as a fresh addition to gastronomic tourism in the region. 🪰

Château Talaud

PHOENIX AMID THE VINES

Château Talaud is in the Comtat Venaissin region of Vaucluse—the ancient papal territory surrounding the town of Carpentras between the banks of the Rhône and Mont Ventoux, where Pope Clement V transferred from Rome in the fourteenth century.

The village of Loriol-du-Comtat is on the road from Orange to Carpentras, amidst Côtes de Ventoux vineyards and close by the Côtes du Rhône *grands crus* of Châteauneuf-du-Pape and Gigondas. Talaud is secluded at the end of a tree-lined avenue, its pale gold facade and terracotta roof contrasting harmoniously with the azure Provençal sky.

The Marquis Grille l'Estoublen built the classical château in 1732 and his coat of arms is a central motif in elegant stonework ornamenting the entrance. Talaud is one of few châteaus in the region, and the proprietors have revived its splendor with style and sensitivity. Conny and Hein Dieters-Kommer, originally from Holland, epitomize cosmopolitan sophistication; they are exceptionally well traveled, sharing six languages and international business experience between Boston, Geneva, Moscow, and Lyon. Fixed on the dream of creating a family B&B offering the personalized welcome they experienced at New England inns, the Dieters-Kommers came upon Talaud and its 74-acre estate languishing in neglect but with enormous potential. Many of the property's distinguished architectectural features— courtyard entry grille, fountain basin, stone archway, and spring-fed "pool"—are registered as protected monuments.

Conny & Hein Dieters-Kommer's
COUPS DE COEUR

Le Jardin du Quai Restaurant
This is a popular canteen for nearby l'Isle-sur-la-Sorgue antique dealers. With garden tables available, the welcome is friendly and the satisfying cuisine rarely disappoints.

Gallery Lysiane Roche, L'Isle sur-la-Sorgue
Roche's exquisite taste ensures a marvelous selection of Art Deco objects and furniture.

Chez Serge
Serge is a minor celebrity in Carpentras and you might spot Patricia Wells at his lively bistro off the town square, under the ancient tree in the courtyard dining room. Serge also conducts wine tours.

Pâtisserie Jouvaud
Operating since 1951, this family bakery in Carpentras prides itself on sticking to artisanal methods using the best local ingredients. They propose sweet and savory as well as chocolate. Everything is as good as it looks and may be sampled in the tea salon.

Domaine de la Marotte
Daan and Elvira van Dikman are enthusiastic young Dutch vintners. Their family purchased the vineyard in 1987, and it is now producing four reds, two whites, and a popular rosé—Le Rose de Marotte—produced from the Bandol grape Mourvèdre. It has hints of strawberry and raspberry and keeps for two to three years.

Conny has designed an environment where guests quickly relax and settle in. "Creating a château d'hôte isn't just about decorating a place and filling it with antiques; it's giving your guests a home away from home," she says.

J'ESSAIE DE TRAVAILLER

Listed elements of the interior are the central stairwell and fresco medallions of cherubs in the first-floor guest rooms.

Conny's past hotel management experience, while less hands-on than her current activity, honed an organizational skill evident at Talaud. Exuding efficiency, Conny whips up a buffet breakfast laid out in the entry hall, where guests help themselves to a cornucopia of treats, before settling at a garden table in the *cour d'honneur* (front courtyard), which serves as the château's warm-weather salon. The casual chic of this outdoor living space is emblematic of Talaud's low-key refinement. While the classic beauty of the building and its surroundings impart a degree of formality, Conny has designed an environment where guests quickly relax and settle in. "Creating a *château d'hôte* isn't just about decorating a place and filling it with antiques, it's giving your guests a home away from home," she says.

Table d'hôte dinner is served twice weekly, either in the gracious dining room or in the pergola-covered veranda overlooking the vineyards. The Provençal cuisine reflects the ready availability of outstanding produce in this sun-drenched region.

While Conny manages the B&B, Hein oversees the impeccable gardens and vineyards that produce 70,000 bottles of award-winning Côtes de Ventoux. The château gardens are bordered front and back by vines,

expanded and replanted by Hein, which now cover half the estate. Hein's cautious development strategy has been rewarded with a steady accumulation of regional and national medals, including a gold from the Côtes de Ventoux Syndicat and a bronze at the prestigious Concours Général d'Agricole de Paris in 2003. His Cuvée 2001 red rates a double *coup de coeur* in the 2004 Hachette wine guide. Says Hein, "I took my time developing quality wine that has achieved recognition winning tasting medals and is gaining word of mouth. I'm not interested in making wine for supermarket distribution."

Dynamic Conny is similarly emphatic about controlling the character of the B&B. "There is a two-night minimum because we don't want to be a *hôtel de passage*. Provence is a destination, not a stopover." If anything, the couple's problem became finding a solution for guests who wish to extend their visit for a week or longer, to shop the markets and to experiment with some of their own cooking. Two weekly rental self-catering villas have been renovated adjacent to the main house. The Petit Talaud sleeps up to six and is a fun base for guests who visit for the fall *vendanges* (grape harvest). This season offers a unique opportunity to experience authentic rural traditions. Guests may fall into bed exhausted, but are certain to leave with exhilarating memories of their time in Provence. 🗡

Château La Roque

ROOMS WITH A VIEW

Perched on a rock face in the foothills of the Vaucluse Plateau overlooking the terraced village of La Roque-sur-Pernes with landscape extending to infinity, La Roque offers some of the loveliest views in Provence. It is a destination for lovers and those in need of salving their spirits contemplating the beauty of nature under the shade of an olive tree with *cigales* (cicadas) serenading.

A fortified structure has existed on the site for one thousand years. The current restored château is the vestige of an eleventh-century fortress, which served as a citadel-sanctuary for the village against waves of invasion. Its four towers and feudal keep were demolished in 1250 under order of the pope and the French king at the Siege of Avignon, to punish the rebellious Count of Toulouse. The property fell into church hands, where its strategic value was its elevated situation on the frontier of papal territory. La Roque was successively pledged to loyal aristocrats, until converting to a private domain in the eighteenth century.

The proprietors, the Tomasinos, have carefully preserved the fortress's character. Each room has a distinct medieval architectural element and the mood throughout is one of monastic purity. The clean lines of the stonework are complemented by sophisticated but restrained decor. Contemporary lighting designers were commissioned to create custom light fixtures for each room, which add a fanciful touch. Rooms are furnished with pieces from Paris and neighboring l'Isle-

Chantal & Jean Tomasino's
COUPS DE COEUR

Fête du Patrimoine,
Pernes-Les-Fontaines

Every third weekend of September the town famed for its forty fountains is a hive of activity. This festival celebrates local culture and traditions and features craft demonstrations, folk dancing, all manner of exhibitions, and endless excuses to snack.

Sénanque Abbey, Gordes

An active Cistercian community is installed in this Romanesque monument founded in 1148. Situated in a narrow valley, the church faces north rather than east so that light enters during mass. The monks cultivate lavender and honey to fund ongoing restoration.

Road from Venasque
to Sénanque

Venasque is rated one of France's most beautiful villages for its architectural unity and sublime site on a cliff with a view of Mont Ventoux and surrounded by scrubland, vines, and cherry trees. The route to the town of Gordes is one of the region's most scenic.

Vignobles Brunier,
Châteauneuf-du-Pape

The Brunier family, owner of Le Vieux Télégraphe, have been producing fine wine since 1898. The fourth generation has expanded holdings to Domaine La Roquette and Les Pallières in neighboring Gigondas.

Sylvain Frères,
Paysans *Nougatiers*

Pierre and Philippe Sylvan craft their high-quality nougat the old-fashioned way from honey, almonds, and fruit they produce themselves. The specialty at their shop Saint Didier is "black" nougat made with caramelized honey.

sur-la-Sorgue, Provence's antiques mecca.

Chantal and Jean Tomasino fell for La Roque because it corresponded exactly to their wish list. "We wanted a place with three essential qualities—high elevation, private, and with soul—but it was the view and medieval architecture that seduced us," recalls Jean. Being an amateur historian, he has extensively researched his home's past and is ready to respond to the curious with impressive detail. As with many *château d'hôte* proprietors, the couple's B&B activity is augmented by freelance careers. They are part of a new wave of urbanites who are shifting their primary residence to

the country, thanks to rapid transportation networks created by regional low-cost airlines and the TGV. Because of La Roque's

proximity to the Avignon TGV station, the Tomasinos can travel back and forth to Paris with ease. Chantal spends a few days every week in the capital for her job as a consultant for an American strategic human resources firm. Jean is able to work at home overseeing regional and community development projects for state bank Caisse des Dépôts.

Jean is passionate about regional gastronomy and has researched local producers to develop a program of tours and tastings to initiate visitors to the finest wines, open-air markets, and gastronomic resources. He organizes tasting weekends—hosted by Christopher Tassin, who was voted France's best sommelier in 2004—where guests visit selected southern Rhône Valley, Ventoux, and Luberon vintners.

Besides convenient proximity to Avignon and l'Isle-sur-la-Sorgue, La Roque also is close to Ventoux villages that have retained a timeless charm, like Saint Didier and Pernes-Les-Fontaines. The landscape of Ventoux, characterized by hills and steep valleys, offers remarkable variety. Cresting the top of a hill, the countryside can abruptly change and is wilder than the plains of Luberon. Tourism is an important economic component for Ventoux, but agriculture remains a thriving sector that sustains villages as vibrant year-round communities.

The rocky terrain, with its shallow topsoil warmed by prevailing sunshine, is ideal for the cultivation of cherries, melons, and strawberries. Truffles are also a major crop. Despite the common name "Périgord" truffle, 35 percent of the world supply actually originates from Vaucluse. National prices are established in November at the Carpentras Friday truffle market.

You won't find acres of lawn or manicured flowerbeds at La Roque, but a series of intimate terraced gardens planted with indigenous flowering plants, fragrant herbs (*senteurs*), and graceful trees are just right for reading or basking in dappled sunshine. The main terrace has a dining table shaded by a grape arbor. It is a natural gathering place, though the view through trailing vines risks upstaging the most scintillating conversation.

Auberge de l'Aiguebrun

NESTING DOWN BY THE RIVER

Tucked into a secluded valley is Sylvia Buzier's cozy sanctuary where guests alight to smooth their rumpled travel feathers on a hillside sloping down to the sparkling Aiguebrun River. The beguiling inn is off a scenic road that cuts across the Luberon Mountains between the village of Bonnieux and the Château de Lourmarin. Terraced villages, valleys, and ravines characterize this corner of Petit Luberon. The property has the environmental advantage of being within Luberon National Park, which keeps wildlife abundant and development at bay.

The bustling Sylvia is of that breed of preening but practical Frenchwoman who look fetching at all hours while delving into every detail of the household with a hawkish eye for standards. Sylvia was an urbanite in her prior life, running the successful Auberge de la Treille in Avignon, but she fell in love and escaped the city with partner Francis Motta, a gentle man who happens to be a dynamite chef.

Animal lovers are in their element at Aiguebrun, since Sylvia indulges an affinity for animals in general and feathered creatures in particular. There are several docile dogs ruled by an imperious goose, strutting peacocks, an aviary of fragile canaries, dozens of ducks, a greenhouse with slumbering cats, an enclosure with a goat and shy sheep, plus the henhouse where free-range chickens lay eggs for the kitchen.

The ambiance is country cottage, Provence-style, and the premiere space is a sunny dining room entered by passing

Sylvia Buzier's
COUPS DE COEUR

The River
Provence is so habitually dry that Sylvia immediately fell in love with the property when she spotted the river.

La Fenière Restaurant, Lourmarin
Reine and Guy Sammut are good friends of Sylvia. The exceptional cuisine in their long-established restaurant continues to win guide-book accolades.

Nougat & Lavender, Sault
Trek to the northeast corner of Vaucluse for André Boyer, who makes the world's finest nougat. The family has remained master nougatiers since 1887. Try the brioche with red praline. Nicknamed "capital of lavender," the town of Sault has a major cooperative and distillery.

Old Rock Shelter
An ancient site on the property marked by an oak with a double trunk, it once served as refuge for the former hamlet during the religious wars. The spot has a karmic aura and is warmed perpetually by the sun.

Cedar Forest, Bonnieux
Sylvia loves to walk the trails in this nearby nature preserve. It is one of the highlights of the Luberon Regional Park, which covers over 408,000 acres of the Vaucluse and Alpes de Haute Provence departments.

through the former back door. It is actually a solidly enclosed porch overlooking the stone-hewn semicircular terrace and the river beyond. Meals are served on the outdoor terrace in fine weather at stone-topped tables ringing the low wall. The restaurant at Aiguebrun is a justifiable draw. Sylvia and Francis collaborate on a flavorful menu featuring organic ingredients from their kitchen garden and the insider network of regional suppliers they've developed. Francis's part Italian heritage is a subtle influence, and the wine on offer includes a careful selection of excellent

local reds such as Château la Canorgue–Côtes de Luberon, which garnered a gold medal in 2003 at the Paris Concours Général Agricole.

Guest rooms are simply furnished in a consciously pared-down country manner. Sylvia has a stylist's instinct and though she strives for natural effect, no detail is haphazard. Her penchant for white-on-white bathrooms is refreshingly crisp. An unexpected accommodation option is adorable cabins strung along the bank of the river. It's part North American lakeside, part Swiss chalet, with a little porch equipped with comfortable chairs and a table. The interiors are chic and cheerful, with clever attention to detail. The concept evolved from a need to expand while respecting stringent zoning, and the solution is as whimsical as it is eco-friendly. Proximity to the pool is a plus, with guests able to enjoy a morning swim just by slipping out in their terry robes before dressing for the day.

Hiking paths radiate into the woods for a brisk walk before the delectable breakfast. Homemade croissants and yogurt with a *coulis* of garden berries are two of numerous temptations. A still life of apothecary jars filled with varieties of raw sugar, sun-dried raisins, and organic cereals are augmented by crusty wood-fired bread, local honey, and homemade jams to satisfy the health conscious and gourmand alike.

Nostalgia for a region where she vacationed in childhood drew Sylvia back to the Luberon. Her quest for refined rusticity and fundamental pleasures imbues Aiguebrun with true escapist charm.

Château d'Esparron

HIGHLANDS IN PROVENCE

Esparron is at the southern limit of Alpes de Haute Provence, where Lac Esparron flows into the canyons of the Basses Gorges du Verdon. These foothills of the Alps have some of the most dramatic scenery and purest air in Provence. The craggy terrain is carpeted with green oak and pine. Nights can be cool even at height of summer.

A château has overlooked the lake since the Castellane family first implanted a fortress in 1218. The imposing square tower of the original construction remains, while the château was gradually transformed in a composite of styles through the nineteenth century. The current owners are progressively restoring it and have done a fine job with the tower, eighteenth-century building, and grounds. Count Bernard is the thirty-first generation and the last remaining branch of the Castellane family to inhabit the region. He inherited the property in 1989 from an uncle without a male heir. Bernard and Charlotte Anne's eldest son, Boniface, bears the name of ancestors who were the last of Provence's mighty independent feudal lords.

If the castle and setting create an impression of being on a loch in the Highlands, Bernard chose his partner well. Charlotte Anne is a fair-haired Scottish native, who especially appreciates her adoptive home in winter: "I love the hard frosts and crystalline sky…when the earth is red and snow caps the peaks. It can get down to minus fifteen at night but it's beautifully crisp and clear."

Esparron has the best qualities of a family home. The three bilingual young Castellanes seem to thrive in the remote

Charlotte Anne & Bernard de Castellane's
COUPS DE COEUR

Musée de la Faience Ancienne, Moustiers

Before stocking up at boutiques offering reproductions of seventeenth- and eighteenth-century designs, train your eye to appreciate the real thing at the Faience Museum.

St Jurs

Nestled against the cliffs north of Moustiers, this micro village dominates the plateau of Vansole. When the mistral blows, visibility is so sharp you can clearly spy Mont Sainte-Victoire at Aix to the south, the Luberon mountain range to the west, and the Alps to the north. A good restaurant is the Deux Nimes.

Rougon

Escape tourist gridlock on the Grand Canyon road in high season by breaking off north past Palud to Rougon, a village seemingly at the end of the earth. Eagles soar above the precipitous peaks in the solitude of a mineral landscape. Recover from your emotions over a savory meal at the Perroquet Vert in La Palud-sur-Verdon.

Ruiz Market

Open Wednesday and Saturday mornings, Ruiz hasn't sold its soul to tourism and remains active year round. Don't be dissuaded by crowds—the ancient streets with Renaissance facades are worth exploring.

but bracing environment. The residential part of the house is the harmonious eighteenth-century wing, which leads to the entry court and countryside. The front door is reached by going up a stately sweep of steps. The château is at the crest of the village, and a view from a flower-filled terrace garden, at the far side of the interior courtyard, overlooks the church and quaint houses.

The nearby Gorges du Verdon is France's Grand Canyon and eminently worth an excursion. The river appears sea green from the heights, and the expanse of Lac de Sainte Croix is astonishing. The region was recently designated a protected national park, and the drive

to the Verdon Grand Canyon takes you across one of its principal features—the plateau of Valensole (the largest in Europe). The wide-

open landmass is abloom with lavender in July. The purple fields juxtaposed with brick-red earth and mountainous horizon are stunning.

The area is an outdoor sports enthusiast's dream, with opportunities for myriad water activities, plus climbing, hiking, and cycling. There are also enchanting historic villages and monuments to explore. A celebrated village is Moustiers-Sainte-Marie, founded by monks in the fifth century. As one approaches from the valley below, the village appears to magically emerge from the rocks. Renowned for its faience potters, Moustiers also has an excellent hotel-restaurant owned by chef Alain Ducasse. Charlotte Anne heartily recommends the table at La Bastide de Moustiers, where a decorative vegetable garden supplies the kitchen.

Guest rooms at Esparron are on two floors of the eighteenth-century wing, reached via the tower's broad spiral staircase. The ambiance is light and spacious, with high molded ceilings, marble fireplaces, and family antiques. A genteel whiff of Scottish country manor can be detected in the unadorned elegance of the teakettle and fixings set out on a tray. The view takes in ponies grazing the hillside through a curtain of plane trees and a splashing fountain beyond the entry gate. Plans are in place to furnish a casual guest sitting room with a television, since the two reception rooms, while lovely, are less suited for children and relaxed gatherings than for an after-dinner drink.

Breakfast is served in the vaulted kitchen, where a generous buffet is laid out and guests settle around the homey oak table. The open fireplace and traditional *potager*-style oven, once fed by embers, are reminders of how labor-intensive cooking remained until this century.

A suggested detour is a trip to the top of the keep for a panoramic view of the lake and village. Deep crenulations keep vertigo at bay and the route up via the castle's ancient innards is fascinating.

Bernard and Charlotte Anne are natural hosts with an infectious passion for the singular legacy of their home. Their enthusiasm for the region is equally sincere and they readily share their experience to ensure that visitors profit from all its wonders.

Le Mas de Peint

REGAL RANCHING IN CAMARGUE

If Texas may be considered a country unto itself, Camargue is its French equivalent. Both have cowboy cultures, proud temperaments, and enduring traditions that don't necessarily migrate well. Cowboy boots don't make it in Manhattan any better than the Provençal print *gardian* shirt passes muster in Paris, except on a gypsy guitarist.

Situated in the Bouches-du-Rhône department, Camargue is an alluvial plain in the delta of marshland below the city of Arles, where the Rhône River forks into the Petit and Grand Rhône, en route to the Mediterranean. Its heart is the vast "pond," the Etang de Vaccares, which flows into a lacework of smaller ponds and coastal islands roped off from the sea by a narrow strip of land. Protected as a zoological and botanical nature preserve, the Camargue Natural Regional Park (as it is officially known) is among the best places in France for bird-watching, with over 400 species sighted, including 160 migratory species. The marshy plains are home to an indigenous race of small white horses, which have been domesticated by ranchers for herding native bulls.

Bull culture (*tauromachie*) is a predominant component of local tradition. It encompasses bull-fighting (*corrida*) and bloodless bull racing (*la course à la cocarde*). Black Camargue bulls are lithe, with distinctive lyre-shaped horns. Their natural agility makes them especially well suited for traditional *cocarde* races. Prime *tauromachie* events take place at the ancient arena in Arles and the small coastal town of Stes-Maires-de-la-Mer (a gypsy pilgrimage destination). Easter

204

Lucille and Jacques Bon's
COUPS DE COEUR

La Digue à la Mer

*Standing on the narrow strip of land
known as "le bout du monde"—the
barrier dividing marshland and sea—one
gets a true sense of how Camargue is
composed of water with just a bit of earth.*

Sunset on the Etang
du Vaccarès

*Here you'll find a magnificent color show,
especially in winter when the mistral is
blowing. Each season is different, with its
particular sights and sounds.*

Nature Watch

*Wander the small roads around the Mas
late in the day to observe the animals. If
you are quiet and still they will approach.*

Musée de l'Arles antique

*This modern triangular blue structure
alongside the Rhône River houses an
extensive collection of Arlesian antiquities,
formerly dispersed throughout the city.
It creates a vivid portrait of Arles in the
era of the Roman Empire.*

Place du Forum, Arles

*An ideal spot to sit and enjoy a coffee
on a pleasant day, absorbing the tempo
of the city.*

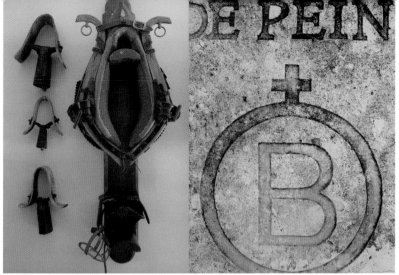

weekend (*ferias de Pâques*) and the second weekend of September (*ferias du riz*) are big *corrida* festivals, while for *cocarde* afficionados, May Day (*Fête des Gardians*) and the *Cocarde d'Or* in July are highlights of the April through October racing season.

Jacques Bon, sheep-farmer-turned-rancher and owner of Le Mas de Peint, is every inch the lean, lanky cowboy. Defying his approaching eighty years, he exudes loose-limbed charm and the disarming grace of a man attuned to the subtle signs of nature. A maverick who embraces risk, Jacques is proud to have transformed the 1,360-acre family farm into a diversified

business, incorporating organic rice production, a *manade* (herd) of 300 bulls, forty Camargue horses, a sophisticated inn,

and an arena where bull races are staged for the public.

The Mas, which dates from 1602, bears the design imprimatur of Jacques's wife Lucille, the accomplished architect responsible for its renovation ten years ago. Lucille collaborated with a designer on the interior to create decor that manages to feel spare and contemporary while incorporating the right touches of Provençal antiques and regional motifs. Many of the graphic black-and-white photographs in the salon and dining room are vintage shots of Jacques as dashing guardian in traditional costume, or of his daughter, who reigned as Queen of the Guardians in Arles and now, with her brother, runs the luxurious Château des Alpilles hotel in Saint Rémy de Provence, owned by the former Madame Bon. Hospitality and a taste for luxury are evidently Bon family traits.

Lucille and Jacques's twenty-year-old son Frédérique is in training to take on the family estate, much as Jacques did from his father, whose brand—a "B" encircled with a small cross on its circumference—is a recurring emblem on everything from embroidered linen sheets to the hindquarters of the herd.

The cuisine at Le Mas de Peint is high caliber, and the fixed dinner menu favors regional recipes with farm-fresh ingredients and local catch. Guests eat at individual tables in the atmospheric kitchen-dining room, where the chef fires up dishes (after preparation is completed in an adjoin-

ing kitchen) and the Bons make a point of stopping by to chat with guests. Jacques has no illusion that Camargue is for everyone—mosquitoes can be irritating and locals are not famously welcoming. "Visitors who come here discover a mysterious land and leave either loving it or hating it," he admits with a shrug.

Observers of the natural world are likely to be captivated. Penetrating the Camargue is best achieved in the saddle or the seat of a four-wheel-drive vehicle. Both options are readily available and when coaxed, Jacques may be persuaded to act as a guide. Camargue horses are mounted western style and don't demand serious equestrian experience. The saddle cradles the rider, and stirrups are worn so that one is virtually standing—a position suited to walking and gentle cantering, since trotting is neither a Camargue horse's natural gait, nor adequately cushioned by the traditional saddle. Any discomfort is compensated for by the thrill of playing cowboy among tamer females with their calves or observing abundant flora and fauna covering the wild plains bordered by shallow canals (*roubines*).

For those preferring a less strenuous program, a fresh salad served at poolside is a tempting midday option along with a stroll through the gardens to admire the roses and sample the bounty of succulent figs. Whatever your tempo, Le Mas de Peint is a civilized oasis for an escape into nature. 🌾

Château Saint-Maximin

NIGHTS MORE BEAUTIFUL THAN YOUR DAYS

The drive west from Avignon to the village of Saint-Maximin on the outskirts of Uzès passes a marvel of Roman antiquuity—the Pont du Gard—a preserved segment of the first-century aqueduct that once channeled spring water from the Eure River south to the city of Nîmes. This aesthetic and engineering marvel soars 44 yards above the waters of the Gardon, the harmony of its running tiers of stone arcades silhouetted against the rugged beauty of the Mediterranean landscape.

"French Tuscany," as this region is known, is redolent with history. There is a timeless character to the narrow, shady streets of its towns and villages set against vineyards, olive groves, and cypress and fig trees.

As in an urban Italian villa, the hidden charm of Le Château de Saint-Maximin is sequestered within the cool confines of its ochre walls. Beyond the Renaissance edifice is a private Alhambra of sun and shadow gardens, with goldfish glinting in the antique basin of a splashing fountain and an emerald swimming pool discreetly tucked within an elevated terrace. The entrance leads into a vaulted stone salon open at one side to the garden, where guests escape the midday sun contemplating the play of light on mullioned windows and twisting pillars, or dine with a view of the stars.

The twelfth-century medieval fortress was transformed extensively in the seventeenth century. Present at the time was the young poet Racine, exiled from Paris by parents hoping his uncle, vicar of Uzès, could prove an edifying

Alain Manière & Jean-Marc Perry's COUPS DE COEUR

Hot-Air Ballooning at Dawn
Take off at first light in a montgolfière when the wind is still, and witness the gentle awakening of the garrigue (scrubland).

Organic Market, Uzès
The market is open on Wednesday mornings. Try a taste of Pelardons des Cevennes, a little goat cheese with hints of honey.

Chabrier Brothers
This modest vineyard in the village of Bourdic offers tastings of local vintages from the barrel before they are bottled.

Corrida on Horseback with the Master Mendozza
Go to the cities of Nîmes or Arles and watch an awesome demonstration of equestrian art in the arena by this great bullfighter— a rare fusion of man and horse.

Sunset, Pont du Gard
Relish a bottle of vintage champagne with a loved one while the sun goes down over an incomparable landmark.

influence. The tone of Racine's *Lettres d'Uzès* implies that an irrepressible sensuality undermined any clerical calling. An oft-quoted poem eulogizing the region concludes with: "...*nous avons des nuits plus belles que vos jours*" ("our nights are more beautiful than your days").

Alain Manière (son of celebrated chef Jacques) and Franco-Irish partner Jean-Marc Perry were proprietors of the stylish "55"—Paris' first *chambre d'hôte* establishment, in a Corbusier building with Art Deco furnishings. Their southern *château d'hote* followed in 1999. Jean-Marc is a

hands-on host and is responsible for the eclectic decor blending contemporary art with provincial, Deco, and contemporary furnishings. Jean-Marc's design flair is ebullient to match his sunny, outgoing personality. A former top model and dancer turned entrepreneur, he glows with health and optimism. Staff is treated like family and is consequently warm and helpful.

Jean-Marc's chief source of pride is charismatic young chef Lisa Muncan, voted best chef graduate of Denmark's leading culinary hotel school. Lisa found her way here via Rome, where the Danish ambassador invited her to run the embassy kitchen. Lisa's Gypsy heritage and Danish upbringing are liberating culinary influences: she isn't bogged down in tradition and has Scandinavian rigor about sourcing organic ingredients. Jean-Marc is amazed how local suppliers plant things especially for her.

Thanks to an exchange arrangement with her former school, Danish graduates with like-minded culinary training assist Lisa. "I took the job at the château because they agreed to let me move beyond a traditional provincial menu. I do what I feel—not fusion but a free-minded approach with emphasis on enhancing flavors. There's a special spirit here—we have fun cooking."

The press has taken note, and success has meant opening the restaurant to nonresidents, though numbers are limited by the intimate size of the dining room. Diners luxuriate in tobacco leather club chairs in a vaulted medieval interior that includes a twelfth-century well.

The cocooning environment at Saint Maximin is conducive to lingering over a delightful breakfast prepared by ever-agreeable Rashida in the *senteur* (herb) garden, planted atop a former medieval tower. The olive trees are reputed to be more than five hundred years old—testimony to how beneficial the aura is. To assuage twinges of sedentary guilt, there is a fitness center and hammam spa where restorative Oriental body treatments and massage are available.

Most featured properties are family homes, so be sure to check websites for possible modifications to opening dates. While many receive guests year-round, some of the B&Bs are open only in high season, which generally runs from April 1 through October. In some instances, a minimum stay of two nights is required. Because the number of rooms is limited, advance booking is recommended, particularly in high season and for groups. Many of the properties are ideal locations for a wedding reception, milestone birthday celebration, or family reunion. Consult websites for details regarding catering services.

Rate

Moderate corresponds to room rates ranging between 70 and 150 euros for a double. The charge is sometimes lower for a single person.

Luxury corresponds to room rates ranging between 120 and 300 euros for a double. Most properties in this category have suite accommodations.

All properties have en suite private bathrooms. Consult websites for complete list of rates and services.

Meals

Table d'hôtes should be reserved in advance, particularly if you wish to dine the evening of your arrival. In high season, table d'hôtes are offered most evenings, or scheduled for specific evenings. The table d'hôte is always a fixed menu, so notify your hosts of any dietary restrictions in advance. Some menus are inclusive of drinks; others charge à la carte for wine and beverages. Breakfast tends to be included at properties in the moderate price range and is usually an additional charge per person at luxury properties.

BRITTANY

CHÂTEAU DE GUILGUIFFIN

29710 Landudec
Philippe and Angelika Davy
TEL: 33 (0) 2 98 91 52 11
FAX: 33 (0) 2 98 91 52 52
chateau@guilguiffin.com
www.guilguiffin.com
RATE: luxury
MEALS: breakfast (included)
OPEN: year-round

CHÂTEAU DE TALHOUËT

56220 Rochefort-en-Terre
Jean-Pol Soulaine
TEL: 33 (0) 2 97 43 34 72
FAX: 33 (0) 2 97 43 35 04
chateaudetalhouet@libertysurf.fr
www.chateaudetalhouet.com
RATE: luxury
MEALS: breakfast (included),
    dinner (extra)
OPEN: year-round

Coups de coeur

LES REMPARTS antique shop
21, rue F. Decker
5600 Vannes
TEL: 33 (0) 2 97 47 46 10

KEROUZINE cheese shop
Place du Poids Public
5600 Vannes

CHÂTEAU ET JARDINS DE LA BALLUE

35560 Bazouges-la-Pérouse
Marie-France Barrère and
    Alain Schrotter
TEL: 33 (0) 2 99 97 47 86
FAX: 33 (0) 2 99 97 47 70
alain.schrotter@wanadoo.fr
www.la-ballue.com
RATE: luxury
ROOMS: 3 doubles, 1 triple, 1 suite
MEALS: breakfast (extra),
    light dinner (extra)
OPEN: March 1–October 31

Coups de coeur

OLIVIER ROELLINGER restaurant
1, rue Duguesclin, Cancale
TEL: 33 (0) 2 99 89 64 76
maisons-de-bricourt.com

LIEU-DIT ART GALLERY
Saint Symphorien
35630 Hédé
TEL/FAX: 33 (0) 2 99 45 51 59
beauchamps.pascale@wanadoo.fr

NORMANDY

MANOIR DE THIONVILLE

14710 Colombieres
Nicole and Michel Fernando
TEL/FAX: 33 (0) 2 31 21 35 11
www.manoir-thionville.com
RATE: moderate
ROOMS: 3
MEALS: breakfast (included),
    dinner (extra)
CLOSED: December 15–March 1

Coups de coeur

MAISON GOSSELIN
27, rue Verrue
Saint Vaast La Hougue
TEL: 33 (0) 2 33 54 40 06
www.maison-gosselin.fr

LA MAISON DE SOPHIE

Le Presbytère
14950 St-Étienne-la-Thillaye
Sophie and Jacki Dudemaine
TEL: 33 (0) 2 31 65 69 97
FAX: 33 (0) 2 31 65 69 98
www.lamaisondesophie.fr
RATE: moderate
ROOMS: 5
MEALS: dinner (extra)
OPEN: February–December

Coups de coeur

VAL DE CIMES adventure forest
14130 Saint-Gatien-des-Bois
TEL: 33 (0) 6 30 91 37 96
FAX: 33 (0) 2 32 65 49 96
www.levaldecimes.com

CHÂTEAU DU VENDEUVRE
14170 Vendeuvre
TEL: 33 (0) 2 31 40 93 83

ESCARGOTS DE BROTONNE
Route Hauteville
27350 Rougemontiers
TEL: 33 (0) 2 32 42 89 86

LA FERME DES BRUYÈRES
Benoit Charbonneau
"Les Bruyeres Carre"
14590 Moyaux
TEL: 33 (0) 2 31 62 81 98

LES MILLE FEUILLES

Domaine de la Petite Lande

14290 Cerqueux

Pierre Brinon

TEL/FAX: 33 (0) 2 31 63 89 77

maisondhotes@les-mille-feuilles.com

www.lesmillefeuilles.com/
  maisondhotes.htm

RATE: moderate

MEALS: breakfast (included),
  dinner (extra)

CLOSED: February

Coups de coeur

POISSONERIE "AUGRÉ DES FLOTS"

118 rue Grande

14290 Orbec

TEL: 33 (0) 2 31 32 82 14

CHÂTEAU LA THILLAYE

27450 St-Christophe-sur-Condé

Roxanne Longpré and
  Patrick Matton

TEL: 33 (0) 2 32 56 07 24

FAX: 33 (0) 2 32 56 70 47

chateaulathillaye@wanadoo.fr

www.chateaulathillaye.com

RATE: luxury

ROOMS: 6 rooms, 2 suites

MEALS: breakfast (included),
  dinner (extra)

OPEN: year-round

Coups de coeur

ABBEY OF NOTRE DAME DU BEC

27800 Le Bec-Hellouin

TEL: 33 (0) 2 32 43 72 60

FAX: 33 (0) 2 32 44 96 69

www.abbayedubec.com

CHAMP DE BATAILLE GOLF CLUB

27110 Le Neubourg

TEL: 33 (0) 2 32 35 03 72

FAX: 33 (0) 2 32 35 83 10

www.champdebataille.com

L O I R E

CHÂTEAU DE BRISSAC

(pictured but not profiled)

49320 Brissac-Quincé

Charles-André and Larissa
  de Cossé-Brissac

TEL: 33 (0) 2 41 91 22 21

MEALS: dinner (extra)

OPEN: April–October

CHÂTEAU DES RÉAUX

37140 Chouzé-sur-Loire

The Goupil de Bouillé family

TEL: 33 (0) 2 47 95 14 40

FAX: 33 (0) 2 47 95 18 34

reaux@club-internet.fr

www.chateaureaux.net

RATE: luxury

ROOMS: 5 rooms, 1 suite,
  1 apartment

MEALS: breakfast (extra),
  dinner for groups only (extra)

OPEN: year-round

Coups de coeur

ECOLE NATIONALE
D'EQUITATION

49411 Saumur

TEL: 33 (0) 2 41 53 50 60

OPEN: April–September

CHÂTEAU AND GARDENS
OF VILLANDRY

37510 Villandry

TEL: 33 (0) 2 47 50 02 09

GARDENS OPEN: year-round

CLOSED: mid-November–January

CHÂTEAU DU VAU

37510 Ballan-Miré

Nancy and Bruno Clement

TEL: 33 (0) 2 47 67 84 04

FAX: 33 (0) 2 47 67 55 77

chateauduvau@chez.com

www.chez.com/chateauduvau

RATE: moderate

ROOMS: 5

MEALS: breakfast (included),
  dinner (extra)

OPEN: year-round

Coups de coeur

PRIEURÉ ST-COSME

37520 La Riche-Tours

TEL: 33 (0) 2 47 37 32 70

AUBERGE DU XII SIÈCLE

1, rue du Château

37190 Saché

TEL: 33 (0) 2 47 26 88 77

CHÂTEAU DE GIZEUX

37340 Gizeux

TEL: 33 (0) 2 47 96 50 92

OPEN: June–September

CHÂTEAU DE LANGEAIS

37130 Langeais

TEL: 33 (0) 2 47 96 72 60

OPEN: Year-round

GOLF DE TOURAINE

37510 Ballan-Miré

TEL: 33 (0) 2 47 67 42 28

CHÂTEAU DES ORMEAUX
Route de Noizay, D1. Nazelles-Négron
37530 Amboise
Emmanuel Guenot, Eric Fontbonnat,
   and Dominique Pepiot
TEL: 33 (0) 2 47 23 26 51
CELL: 33 (0) 2 47 23 19 31
contact@chateaudesormeaux.fr
www.chateaudesormeaux.fr
RATE: moderate
ROOMS: 8
MEALS: breakfast (included),
   dinner (extra)
OPEN: year-round

Coups de coeur
CHÂTEAU DE CHENONCEAU
37150 Chenonceaux
TEL: 33 (0) 2 47 23 90 07
chateau.de.chenonceau@wanadoo.fr
www.chateau-de-chenonceau.fr
OPEN: year-round

CHÂTEAU DU CLOS LUCÉ
Parc Leonardo da Vinci
2, rue du Clos Lucé
37400 Amboise
TEL: 33 (0) 2 47 57 00 73
chateau.closluce@wanadoo.fr
www.vinci-closluce.com
OPEN: year-round

AUBERGE DE LA CROIX BLANCHE
Jean Claude and Emmanuelle Sichi
2, avenue de la Loire
41150 Veuves
TEL: 33 (0) 2 54 70 23 80
FAX: 33 (0) 2 54 70 24 38
jean-claude.sichi@wanadoo.fr
OPEN: March–January

GARDENS OF CHÂTEAU VALMER
Chançay, 37210 Vouvray
TEL: 33 (0) 2 47 52 93 12
valmer37@aol.com
www.chateauxcountry.com/
   chateaux/valmer
OPEN: May–September

LE PAVILLON DES LYS
Chef, Sébastien Begouin
9, rue d'Orange
37400 Amboise
TEL: 33 (0) 2 47 30 01 01
FAX: 33 (0) 2 47 30 01 90
pavillondeslys@wanadoo.fr
www.pavillondeslys.com
OPEN: year-round

CHÂTEAU DES BRIOTTIÈRES
49330 Champigné
Hedwige and François de Valbray
TEL: 33 (0) 2 41 42 00 02
FAX: 33 (0) 2 41 42 01 55
briottieres@wanadoo.fr
www.briottieres.com
RATE: moderate to luxury
ROOMS: 10 in château, 5 in *Fruitier*
MEALS: dinner (extra)

Coups de coeur
CHÂTEAU DE SERRANT
Route Nationale
49170 St Georges sur Loire
TEL: 33 (0) 2 41 39 13 01
contactserrant@aol.com
OPEN: March 15–November 15

COINTREAU DISTILLERY AND MUSEUM
49124 St Barthélemyd'Anjou
Angers
TEL: 33 (0) 2 41 31 50 50
www.cointreau.com

ABBAYE SAINT-PIERRE DE SOLESMES
72300 Solesmes
TEL: 33 (0) 2 43 95 03 08
abbaye@solesmes.com
www.solesmes.com

DOMAINE LANGLOIS-CHÂTEAU
3, rue Léopold Palustre
Saint Hilaire-Saint Florent
49400 Saumur
TEL: 33 (0) 2 41 40 21 00
contact@langlois-chateau.fr

CHÂTEAU DE TERNAY
86120 Ternay
Count and Countess Loic
   and Caroline de Ternay
TEL: 33 (0) 5 49 22 97 54
FAX: 33 (0) 5 49 22 34 66
pro@chateau-de-ternay.com
www.chateau-de-ternay.com
RATE: moderate
ROOMS: 3 rooms, 1 suite
MEALS: breakfast (included),
   buffet and dinner (extra)
OPEN: year-round

Coups de coeur
CHÂTEAU DE MONTSOREAU
49730 Montsoreau
TEL: 33 (0) 2 41 67 12 60
CLOSED: mid-November–
   mid-February

CHÂTEAU DE BRÉZÉ
49260 Brézé
TEL: 33 (0) 2 41 51 60 15
OPEN: May–September

VENDÉE

CHÂTEAU DE LA FLOCELLIÈRE
30, rue du Chateau
85700 La Flocellière
Vicomte and Vicomtesse Patrice
	and Erika Vignial
TEL: 33 (0) 2 51 57 22 03
FAX: 33 (0) 2 51 57 75 21
flocelliere.chateau@wanadoo.fr
www.flocellierecastle.com
RATE: luxury
ROOMS: 6 rooms, 1 suite,
	2 apartments
MEALS: breakfast (extra),
	dinner (extra)

> *Coups de coeur*
> DOMAINE DU CLOSEL
> closel@savennieres-closel.com
> www.savennieres-closel.com
>
> CHÂTEAU DE TERRE NEUVE
> 85200 Fontenay-le-Comte
> TEL: 33 (0) 2 02 51 69 41
> FAX: 33 (0) 2 51 50 00 83
> OPEN: May 1–September 30

CHÂTEAU DE SAINT-LOUP
79600 Saint-Loup Lamairé
Count Charles-Henri de Bartillat
TEL: 33 (0) 5 49 64 81 73
FAX: 33 (0) 5 49 64 82 06
st-loup@wanadoo.fr
www.chateaudesaint-loup.com
RATE: luxury
ROOMS: 11 rooms, 2 suites,
	tower for groups
MEALS: breakfast (extra),
	dinner (extra)

> *Coups de coeur*
> HOTEL DE CYGNE restaurant
> 10, rue du Cygne
> 79600 Airvault
> TEL: 33 (0) 5 49 64 70 61
>
> ABBEY OF FONTEVRAUD
> 49590 Fontevraud-l'Abbaye
> TEL: 33 (0) 2 41 51 71 41
> www.abbaye-fontevraud.com
> OPEN: year-round

BERRY

PRIEURÉ D'ORSAN
18170 Maisonnais
Sonia Lessot and Patrice Taravella
TEL: 33 (0) 2 48 56 27 50
FAX: 33 (0) 2 48 56 39 64
prieuredorsan@wanadoo.fr
www.prieuredorsan.com
RATE: luxury
ROOMS: 7
MEALS: breakfast (extra),
	dinner (extra)
OPEN: year-round

> *Coups de coeur*
> L'ASSEMBLÉE DU PLAIX folk festival
> weekend following August 15
>
> CHÂTEAU DU PLAIX
> 18160 Lignières,
> Les Thiaulins de Lignières Association
> TEL: 33 (0) 2 48 60 22 14
>
> ABBATIALE ST-GENÈS
> 18370 Châteaumeillant
>
> PÉPINIÈRE DES PIGEATS
> Marie France and Jean François Sarrault
> 18170 Loyé-sur-Arnon
> TEL: 33 (0) 2 48 96 19 76

PASCAL DESROCHES
18120 Lazenais
TEL: 33 (0) 2 48 51 71 60

FROMAGERIE DES ETANGS
18170 Ardenais
TEL: 33 (0) 2 48 56 38 47

CHÂTEAU DE LA COMMANDERIE
Farges Allichamps
18200 Saint-Amand-Montrond
Laura and Umberto Ronsisvale
TEL: 33 (0) 2 48 61 04 19
FAX: 33 (0) 2 48 61 01 84
chateaudelacommanderie@wanadoo.fr
www.chateaudelacommanderie.com
RATE: luxury
ROOMS: 8
MEALS: dinner (extra)
OPEN: year-round

> *Coups de coeur*
> PARC FLORAL
> Le Bourg
> 18150 Apremont-sur-Allier
> TEL: 33 (0) 2 48 77 55 06
> apremont-sur-allier@wanadoo.fr
> www.apremont-sur-allier.com
> OPEN: daily from Easter–
> 	September 30
>
> L'ABBAYE DE NOIRLAC
> 18200 Bruère-Alichamps
> TEL: 33 (0) 2 48 62 01 01
> infos@abbayedenoirlac.com
> www.abbayedenoirlac.com
> OPEN: daily from February 1–
> 	December 22

DORDOGNE & AQUITAINE

LE DOMAINE DE SAINT GÉRY
46800 Lascabannes
Pascale and Patrick Duler
TEL: 33 (0) 5 65 31 82 51
FAX: 33 (0) 5 65 22 92 89
infos@saint-gery.com
www.saint-gery.com
RATE: luxury
ROOMS: 4 rooms, 1 suite
MEALS: dinner (extra)
OPEN: May 14–September 13

Coups de coeur
WELLS OF AUJOLS
46090 Aujols

FAÏENCERIE DURAN
12, avenue des Pyrenees
31220
Martres Tolosane
TEL: 33 (0) 5 61 98 84 44
FAX: 33 (0) 5 61 98 88 13

DIDIER SOLIGON,
    IRONMONGER
82110 Lauzerte
TEL: 33 (0) 5 63 94 76 39
CELL: 33 (0) 6 89 53 75 92

ÉGLISE DE LACHAPELLE
82120 Lachapelle
assolachapelle@hotmail.com
www.info82.com/lachapelle
TEL: 33 (0) 5 63 94 12 28
OPEN: May 1–October 31
CLOSED: Tuesdays

LE CHÂTEAU DE PUYMARTIN
24200 Sarlat
Comtesse Henri de Montbron
    and Xavier de Montbron
TEL: 33 (0) 5 53 59 29 97
FAX: 33 (0) 5 53 29 87 52
ch.puymartin@voila.fr
RATE: moderate
ROOMS: 2
MEALS: breakfast (included)
OPEN: April–September

Coups de coeur
THE SUSPENDED GARDENS OF
    MARQUEYSSAC
24220 Vézac
TEL: 33 (0) 5 53 31 36 36
FAX: 33 (0) 5 53 31 36 30
jardins@marqueyssac.com
www.marqueyssac.com
OPEN: year-round

AMMEUBLEMENT ROUCHON
34, rue Republique
24200 Sarlat
TEL: 33 (0) 5 53 59 04 32

CHÂTEAU DE FÉNELON
24370 Sainte Mondane
TEL: 33 (0) 5 53 29 81 45
FAX: 33 (0) 5 53 29 88 99
bestofperigord@perigord.com
www.best-of-perigord.tm.fr
OPEN: year-round

CHÂTEAU DE COMMARQUE
24020 Les Eyzies
TEL: 33 (0) 5 53 59 00 25
FAX: 33 (0) 5 53 28 94 94
www.commarque.com
OPEN: April–September

CINEMA REX, SARLAT
TEL: 33 (0) 8 92 68 69 24

CHÂTEAU DE LA BOURGONIE
24480 La Buisson de Cadouin
Count and Countess Hubert and
    Christine de Commarque
CELL: 33 (0) 6 86 89 91 59
TEL: 33 (0) 1 47 58 15 96
FAX: 33 (0) 1 47 59 91 02
info@demeures-de-commarque.com
www.demeures-de-commarque.com
RATE: moderate
ROOMS: 2 rooms, 2 houses
MEALS: breakfast (extra)
OPEN: May 15–November 1

Coups de coeur
L'ESPLANADE RESTAURANT
24250 Domme
TEL: 33 (0) 5 53 28 31 41
CLOSED: December 11–January 2

YVON CHARPENET, IRONSMITH
Route de Temniac
24200 Sarsat
TEL: 33 (0) 5 53 59 19 05

JEAN LACOMBE, FOIE GRAS
Bénivet
24200 St Andre d'Allas
TEL: 33 (0) 5 53 29 67 62

CHARTREUSE DU BIGNAC
Le Bignac
24520 Saint-Nexans
Jean Louis and Brigitte Viargues
TEL: 33 (0) 5 53 22 12 80
FAX: 33 (0) 5 53 22 12 81
info@abignac.com
www.abignac.com
RATE: luxury
ROOMS: 10
MEALS: breakfast (extra),
    dinner (extra)

Coups de coeur

LES JARDINS DE CADIOT
24370 Carlux
TEL/FAX: 33 (0) 5 53 29 81 05
OPEN: May–October

LE CLOÎTRE DES RÉCOLLETS
Quai Salvette
24100 Bergerac
TEL: 33 (0) 5 53 63 57 55
FAX: 33 (0) 5 53 63 01 30
OPEN: year-round

FRANÇOIS, MASTER PÂTISSIER
    AND CHOCOLATIER
5, rue Sainte-Catherine (opposite)
24100 Bergerac
TEL: 33 (0) 5 53 61 92 10

POINT D'ORGUE
13, rue du Mourier
    (near the covered market)
24100 Bergerac
TEL: 33 (0) 5 53 23 72 41

CHÂTEAU BINASSAT
François Jeante
24520 Saint Nexans
TEL: 33 (0) 5 53 61 21 58

CHÂTEAU DE CARBONNEAU

33890 Pessac-sur-Dordogne
Wilfrid and Jaquie Franc de Ferrière
TEL: 33 (0) 5 57 47 46 46
FAX: 33 (0) 5 57 47 42 26
carbonneau@wanadoo.fr
www.chateau-carbonneau.com
RATE: moderate
ROOMS: 6
MEALS: breakfast (included),
    dinner (extra)
CLOSED: late November–mid-March

Coups de coeur

LE CHÂTEAU DE DURAS
47120 Duras
TEL: 33 (0) 5 53 83 77 32
FAX: 33 (0) 5 53 64 97 99
chateau-de-duras@wanadoo.fr
www.chateau-de-duras.com

MOULIN DE MOUSTELAT
33890 Pessac sur Dordogne
TEL: 33 (0) 5 05 57 46 77
b.r.barriere@wanadoo.fr
OPEN: every day by appointment

MARKET AT SAINTE-FOY-LA-GRANDE
www.paysfoyen.com
ot.sainte-foy-la-grande@wanadoo.fr
TEL: 33 (0) 5 57 46 03 00

LES JARDINS DE SARDY
24230 Velines
TEL: 33 (0) 5 53 27 51 45
OPEN: Easter–All Saints Day

CHÂTEAU LAMOTHE
PRINCE NOIR

33450 Saint-Sulpice et Cameyrac
Véronique, Luce, and Jacques Bastide
TEL: 33 (0) 5 56 30 82 16
FAX: 33 (0) 5 56 30 88 33
chat.lamothe@wanadoo.fr
www.chateaux-france.com/
    lamotheprincenoir
RATE: luxury
MEALS: breakfast (included), dinner
    (groups)
OPEN: year-round

Coups de coeur
LE GRAND THÉÂTRE
Place de la Comédie
33000 Bordeaux
www.bordeaux-tourism.com

DIANA CASTEJA AT GALERIE SPIRIT
26 rue Saint-Amand,
33000 Bordeaux
TEL: 33 (0) 5 59 47 24 50
www.diane-casteja.com

CHÂTEAU QUERCY
33330 Vignonet
Stéphane Aplebaum
TEL: 33 (0) 5 57 84 56 07
chateauquercy@wandoo.fr
www.chateau-quercy.com
OPEN: year-round by appointment

LOGIS DE LA CADENE RESTAURANT
3, place du Marche au Bois
33330 Saint-Émilion
TEL: 33 (0) 2 57 24 71 40
FAX: 33 (0) 5 57 74 42 23
CLOSED: December 22–February 1

PROVENCE

LA MAISON DU MOULIN

Petit Cordy
26230 Grignan
Bénédicte and Philippe Appels
TEL: 33 (0) 4 75 46 56 94
info@maisondumoulin.com
www.maisondumoulin.com
RATE: moderate
ROOMS: 4 rooms, 1 cottage
OPEN: year-round

Coups de coeur
LE VIEUX MOULIN, OLIVE OIL PRESS
26110 Mirabel-aux-Barronnies
TEL: 33 (0) 4 75 27 12 02

DOMAINE DE MONTINE
La Grande Tuiliere
26230 Grignan
TEL: 33 (0) 4 75 46 54 21
www.domaine-de-montine.com

ROBERT CANUT'S SANTONS
Quartier les Blanquettes
26790 Tulette
TEL: 33 (0) 4 75 98 36 79

LES ROUTES DE LA LAVANDE
    ASSOCIATION
TEL: 33 (0) 4 75 26 65 91
info@routes-lavande.com
www.routes-lavande.com

L'AUBE SAFRAN
Chemin du Patifiage
84330 Le Barroux
Marie and François Pillet
TEL/FAX: 33 (0) 4 90 62 66 91
CELL: 33 (0) 6 12 17 96 94
contact@aube-safran.com
www.aube-safran.com
RATE: moderate
MEALS: dinner (extra)
OPEN: year-round

Coups de coeur
TERRES DE SOLENCE
Chemin de la Lègue, 84380 Mazan
TEL/FAX: 33 (0) 4 90 60 55 31
solence@free.fr

LE BATELEUR RESTAURANT
1, Place Théodore Aubanel
84110 Vaison a Romaine
TEL: 33 (0) 4 90 36 28 04
OPEN: year-round, 6 days/week
    (in high season)
CLOSED: Monday, Thursday dinner
    and Saturday lunch

XAVIER VIGNON, OENOLOGUE
Chemin de Caromb
84330 Le Barroux
www.xaviervins.com
TEL: 33 (0) 4 90 62 33 44

LA ROVE GOAT CHEESE
Lou Canestéou
84110 Vaison-la-Romaine

CHÂTEAU TALAUD
84870 Loriol du Comtat
Conny and Hein Deiters-Kommer
TEL: 33 (0) 4 90 65 71 00
FAX: 33 (0) 4 90 65 77 93
chateautalaud@infonie.fr
www.chateautalaud.com
RATE: moderate to luxury
ROOMS: 5
MEALS: dinner (extra)
CLOSED: December 15– January 15

Coups de coeur
LE JARDIN DU QUAI RESTAURANT
2, avenue Julien Guigue
L'Isle-sur-la-Sorgue
TEL: 33 (0) 4 90 20 14 98

GALLERY LYSIANE ROCHE
7, avenue des Quatres Otages
L'Isle-sur-la-Sorgue
TEL: 33 (0) 4 90 38 25 79

CHEZ SERGE
90, rue Cottier
84200 Carpentras
TEL: 33 (0) 4 90 63 21 24
www.chezserge.com

JOUVAUD PASTRY SHOP
    AND TEA SALON
Rue de L'Évêché
84200 Carpentras
TEL: 33 (0) 4 90 63 15 38

DOMAINE DE LA MAROTTE
Petit Chemin de Serres
84200 Carpentras-Serres
Daan and Elvira Van Dijkman
TEL: 33 (0) 4 90 63 43 27

CHÂTEAU LA ROQUE
Chemin du Chateau
84210 La-Roque-sur-Pernes
Chantal and Jean Tomasino
TEL: 33 (0) 4 90 61 68 77
FAX: 33 (0) 4 90 61 68 78
chateaularoque@wanadoo.fr
www.chateaularoque.com
RATE: moderate to luxury
ROOMS: 2 rooms, 3 suites
MEALS: breakfast (extra),
    dinner (extra)
OPEN: year-round

Coups de coeur
PERNES-LES-FONTAINES TOWN HALL
(Mairie)
TEL: 33 (0) 4 90 61 45 00
www.ville-pernes-les-fontaines.fr

ABBAYE NOTRE-DAME DE SÉNANQUE
84220 Gordes
TEL: 33 (0) 4 90 72 05 72
FAX: 33 (0) 4 90 72 15 70
www.abbayedesenanque.com

VIGNOBLES BRUNIER
Châteauneuf-du-Pape
3, route de Chateauneuf-du-Pape
84370 Bedarrides
TEL: 33 (0) 4 90 33 00 31
FAX: 33 (0) 4 90 33 18 47
vignobles@brunier.fr
www.vignoblesbrunier.fr

SYLVAIN FRÈRES NOUGAT
288 Route de Pernes
84210 St Didier
Pierre and Philippe Sylvain
TEL: 33 (0) 4 90 66 09 57

AUBERGE DE L'AIGUEBRUN

Domaine de la Tour
84480 Bonnieux
Sylvia Buzier
TEL: 33 (0) 4 90 04 47 00
FAX: 33 (0) 4 90 04 47 01
sylvia.buzier@wanadoo.fr
www.aubergedelaiguebrun.com
RATE: luxury
MEALS: breakfast (included),
    dinner (extra)
OPEN: Easter–October

Coups de coeur

LA FENIÈRE RESTAURANT
Route de Cadenet, D943
84160 Lourmarin
TEL: 33 (0) 4 90 68 11 79
reine@wanadoo.fr

ANDRÉ BOYER NOUGATIER
Rue de la Porte-des-Aires
84390 Sault
TEL: 33 (0) 4 90 64 00 23
infos@nougat-boyer.fr
www.nougat-boyer.fr
CLOSED: mid-January–mid-February

MAISON DES PRODUCTEURS
Route de la Republique
84390 Sault
TEL: 33 (0) 4 90 64 08 98
OPEN: April–October

CEDAR FOREST OF BONNIEUX
Maison du Parc naturel
    régional du Luberon
84400 Apt
TEL: 33 (0) 4 90 04 42 00
www.parcduluberon.com

CHÂTEAU D'ESPARRON

04800 Esparron de Verdon
Bernard and Charlotte Anne de Castellane
TEL: 33 (0) 4 92 77 12 05
FAX: 33 (0) 4 92 77 13 10
chateau@esparron.com
www.esparron.com
RATE: moderate to luxury
ROOMS: 4 rooms, 1 suite
MEALS: breakfast (included)
CLOSED: November 1–Easter

Coups de coeur

MUSÉE DE LA FAÏENCE ANCIENNE
04360 Moustiers-Ste-Marie
TEL: 33 (0) 4 92 74 61 74

DEUX NIMES RESTAURANT
St Jurs
TEL: 33 (0) 4 92 74 30 73

PERROQUET VERT RESTAURANT
La Palud-sur-Verdon
TEL: 33 (0) 4 92 77 33 39

LE MAS DE PEINT

Le Sambuc
13200 Arles
Lucille and Jacques Bon
TEL: 33 (0) 4 90 97 20 62
FAX: 33 (0) 4 90 97 22 20
hotel@masdepeint.net
www.masdepeint.com
RATE: luxury
ROOMS: 8 rooms, 3 suites
MEALS: breakfast (extra),
    lunch (extra), dinner (extra)
CLOSED: November 19–December 19
    and January 10–March 18

Coups de coeur

MUSÉE DE L'ARLES ANTIQUE
TEL: 33 (0) 4 90 18 88 92

CHÂTEAU DE SAINT-MAXIMIN

30700 Saint Maximin
Alain Manière and Jean-Marc Perry
TEL: 33 (0) 4 66 03 44 16
FAX: 33 (0) 4 66 03 44 98
info@chateaustmaximin.com
www.chateaustmaximin.com
RATE: luxury
ROOMS: 4 rooms, 2 suites
MEALS: dinner (extra)
CLOSED: February

Coups de coeur

DOMAINE CHABRIER
domaine.chabrier@terre-net.fr
www.chabrier.fr

BALLOONING
Jean Donnet
Tel: 33 (0) 4 66 37 15 21